MznLnx

Missing Links Exam Preps

Exam Prep for

Financial Accounting

Werner & Jones, 3rd Edition

The MznLnx Exam Prep is your link from the texbook and lecture to your exams.
The MznLnx Exam Preps are unauthorized and comprehensive reviews of your textbooks.

MznLnx

Rico
Publications

Exam Prep for Financial Accounting
3rd Edition
Werner & Jones

Publisher: Raymond Houge
Assistant Editor: Michael Rouger
Text and Cover Designer: Lisa Buckner
Marketing Manager: Sara Swagger
Project Manager, Editorial Production: Jerry Emerson
Art Director: Vernon Lowerui

Product Manager: Dave Mason
Editorial Assitant: Rachel Guzmanji
Pedagogy: Debra Long
Cover Image: Jim Reed/Getty Images
Text and Cover Printer: City Printing, Inc.
Compositor: Media Mix, Inc.

Printed in the United States
ISBN:

For more information about our products, contact us at:
Dave.Mason@RicoPublications.com

For permission to use material from this text or product, submit a request online to:
Dave.Mason@RicoPublications.com

Contents

TO THE STUDENT

COMPREHENSIVE

The *MznLnx* Exam Prep series is designed to help you pass your exams. Editors at MznLnx review your textbooks and then prepare these practice exams to help you master the textbook material. Unlike study guides, workbooks, and practice tests provided by the texbook publisher and textbook authors, *MznLnx* gives you ***all*** of the material in each chapter in exam form, not just samples, so you can be sure to nail your exam.

MECHANICAL

The MznLnx Exam Prep series creates exams that will help you learn the subject matter as well as test you on your understanding. Each question is designed to help you master the concept. Just working through the exams, you gain an understanding of the subject--its a simple mechanical process that produces success.

INTEGRATED STUDY GUIDE AND REVIEW

MznLnx is not just a set of exams designed to test you, its also a comprehensive review of the subject content. Each exam question is also a review of the concept, making sure that you will get the answer correct without having to go to other sources of material. You learn as you go! Its the easiest way to pass an exam.

HUMOR

Studying can be tedious and dry. MznLnx's instructional design includes moderate humor within the exam questions on occassion, to break the tedium and revitalize the brain

1. In economics, _________ or _________ goods or real _________ refers to factors of production used to create goods or services that are not themselves significantly consumed (though they may depreciate) in the production process. _________ goods may be acquired with money or financial _________. In finance and accounting, _________ generally refers to financial wealth, especially that used to start or maintain a business.
   a. Capital
   b. Vyborg Appeal
   c. Screening
   d. Disclosure

2. An _________ is a comprehensive report on a company's activities throughout the preceding year. _________s are intended to give shareholders and other interested persons information about the company's activities and financial performance. Most jurisdictions require companies to prepare and disclose _________s, and many require the _________ to be filed at the company's registry.
   a. AIG
   b. AMEX
   c. ABC Television Network
   d. Annual Report

3. In financial accounting, a _________ or statement of financial position is a summary of a person's or organization's balances. Assets, liabilities and ownership equity are listed as of a specific date, such as the end of its financial year. A _________ is often described as a snapshot of a company's financial condition.
   a. Financial statements
   b. 3M Company
   c. Statement of retained earnings
   d. Balance Sheet

4. _________ is a company's financial statement that indicates how the revenue is transformed into the net income The purpose of the _________ is to show managers and investors whether the company made or lost money during the period being reported.

   The important thing to remember about an _________ is that it represents a period of time.

   a. AIG
   b. Income Statement
   c. AMEX
   d. ABC Television Network

5. The term _________, derived from the distinctive T shape, is frequently used when discussing or analyzing accounting or business transactions. _________s are used to represent general ledger accounts.

Typically one or more Ts are drawn on a white board or blank piece of paper. A general ledger account name or number is then written above each T. Debit entries are recorded on the left side of the 'T' and credit entries are recorded on the right side of the 'T'.

a. BNSF Railway
b. BMC Software, Inc.
c. 3M Company
d. T account

6. An _________ invented by esteemed professor Karen Osterheld is the system of records a business keeps to maintain its accounting system. This includes the purchase, sales, and other financial processes of the business. The purpose of an _________ is to accumulate data and provide decision makers (investors, creditors, and managers) with information to make decision While this was previously a paper-based process, most modern businesses now use accounting software such as UBS, MYOB etc.

a. ABC Television Network
b. AMEX
c. AIG
d. Accounting information system

7. _________ are payments made by a corporation to its shareholder members. It is the portion of corporate profits paid out to stockholders. When a corporation earns a profit or surplus, that money can be put to two uses: it can either be re-invested in the business (called retained earnings), or it can be paid to the shareholders as a dividend.

a. Dividend payout ratio
b. Dividend stripping
c. Dividend yield
d. Dividends

8. In accounting, the _________ is a worksheet listing the balance at a certain date, of each ledger account in two columns, namely debit and credit. Under the double-entry system, in any transaction the total of any debits must equal the total of any credits, so in a _________ the total of the debit side should always be equal to the total of the credit side. The _________ thus serves as a tool to detect errors, which can result in the totals not being equal.

a. Current asset
b. Trial balance
c. Depreciation
d. Bottom line

9. _________ and credit are formal bookkeeping and accounting terms. They are the most fundamental concepts in accounting, representing the two records that one party in a transaction makes on its records, transferring a money balance from one account to another, one representing a reduction of liability or increase in asset, and the other representing a balancing increase in liability or reduction of asset.

Introduction

_________s and credits are a system of notation used in accounting to keep track of money movements (transactions) into and out of an account.

a. Bookkeeping
b. Cookie jar accounting
c. Debit and credit
d. Debit

10. In mathematics _________s are numbers or other things that get multiplied. In particular, see:

- Factorization, the decomposition of an object into a product of other objects
- Integer factorization, the process of breaking down a composite number into smaller non-trivial divisors
- A coefficient
- A divisor of a particular number, or of an element of a monoid
- A von Neumann algebra with a trivial center

In statistics

- _________ analysis is the study of how _________s or certain variables affect variables.

In technology:

- Human _________s, a profession that focuses on how people interact with products, tools, or procedures
- 'Functionality, Application domain, Conditions, Technology, Objects and Responsibility;', In object-oriented programming

In computer science and information technology:

- Authentication _________, a piece of information used to verify a person's identity for security purposes
- _________, a Unix command for numbers factorization
- _________ (programming language), an experimental Forth-like programming language

In television:

- The O'Reilly _________, an American talk show hosted by Bill O'Reilly on Fox News.
- The Krypton _________, a British game show hosted by Gordon Burns, formally on ITV. Also had an American version.

.

a. Valuation
b. The Goodyear Tire ' Rubber Company
c. Merck ' Co., Inc.
d. Factor

11. _________ is equal to the income that a firm has after subtracting costs and expenses from the total revenue. _________ can be distributed among holders of common stock as a dividend or held by the firm as retained earnings.

The items deducted will typically include tax expense, financing expense (interest expense), and minority interest. Likewise, preferred stock dividends will be subtracted too, though they are not an expense.

a. Long-term liabilities
b. Net income
c. Matching principle
d. Generally accepted accounting principles

12. In business and finance accounting, _________ is equal to the gross profit minus overheads minus interest payable plus/minus one off items for a given time period (usually: accounting period.)

A common synonym for '_________' when discussing financial statements (which include a balance sheet and an income statement) is the bottom line. This term results from the traditional appearance of an income statement which shows all allocated revenues and expenses over a specified time period with the resulting summation on the bottom line of the report.

a. Cost of goods sold
b. Net Profit
c. Treasury stock
d. Salvage value

13. A sole _________, or simply _________ is a type of business entity which legally has no separate existence from its owner. Hence, the limitations of liability enjoyed by a corporation and limited liability partnerships do not apply to sole proprietors. All debts of the business are debts of the owner.

a. Safety stock
b. Free cash flow
c. Pre-determined overhead rate
d. Proprietorship

14. A _________ is a type of business entity in which partners (owners) share with each other the profits or losses of the business undertaking in which all have invested. _________s are often favored over corporations for taxation purposes, as the _________ structure does not generally incur a tax on profits before it is distributed to the partners (i.e. there is no dividend tax levied.) However, depending on the _________ structure and the jurisdiction in which it operates, owners of a _________ may be exposed to greater personal liability than they would as shareholders of a corporation.

a. National Information Infrastructure Protection Act
b. Corporate governance
c. Resource Conservation and Recovery Act
d. Partnership

15. _________ is a mathematical science pertaining to the collection, analysis, interpretation or explanation, and presentation of data. It also provides tools for prediction and forecasting based on data. It is applicable to a wide variety of academic disciplines, from the natural and social sciences to the humanities, government and business.

a. Statistics
b. Probability distribution
c. Time series
d. Variance

16. _________ was an American statesman and jurist who shaped American constitutional law and made the Supreme Court a center of power. Marshall was Chief Justice of the United States, serving from February 4, 1801, until his death in 1835. He served in the United States House of Representatives from March 4, 1799, to June 7, 1800, and, under President John Adams, was Secretary of State from June 6, 1800, to March 4, 1801.

a. Alan Greenspan
b. Abby Joseph Cohen
c. Arthur Betz Laffer
d. John Marshall

17. _________ is a concept whereby a person's financial liability is limited to a fixed sum, most commonly the value of a person's investment in a company or partnership with _________. A shareholder in a limited company is not personally liable for any of the debts of the company, other than for the value of his investment in that company. The same is true for the members of a _________ partnership and the limited partners in a limited partnership.

a. Joint venture
b. Due diligence
c. Limited liability
d. Burden of proof

18. A _________ is a partnership in which some or all partners (depending on the jurisdiction) have limited liability. It therefore exhibits elements of partnerships and corporations. In an _________ one partner is not responsible or liable for another partner's misconduct or negligence.

a. Dow Jones ' Company
b. Financial Accounting Standards Board
c. Privately held
d. Limited liability partnership

19. A _________ is a form of partnership similar to a general partnership, except that in addition to one or more general partners (GPs), there are one or more limited partners (_________s.) It is a partnership in which only one partner is required to be a general partner.

The GPs are, in all major respects, in the same legal position as partners in a conventional firm, i.e. they have management control, share the right to use partnership property, share the profits of the firm in predefined proportions, and have joint and several liability for the debts of the partnership.

a. Dow Jones ' Company
b. Debenture
c. Minority interest
d. Limited partnership

20. In financial accounting, a _________ is defined as an obligation of an entity arising from past transactions or events, the settlement of which may result in the transfer or use of assets, provision of services or other yielding of economic benefits in the future.

a. Liability
b. False Claims Act
c. Vested
d. Corporate governance

21. _________ refers to the methods, practices and operations conducted to promote and sustain certain categories of commercial activity. The term is understood to have different specific meanings depending on the context. Merchandise is a sale goods at a store

In marketing, one of the definitions of _________ is the practice in which the brand or image from one product or service is used to sell another.

a. 3M Company
b. BMC Software, Inc.
c. Merchandise
d. Merchandising

22. _________ can be regarded as an outcome of mental processes (cognitive process) leading to the selection of a course of action among several alternatives. Every _________ process produces a final choice. The output can be an action or an opinion of choice.

a. Decision making
b. BNSF Railway
c. BMC Software, Inc.
d. 3M Company

23. The _________ is a trilateral trade bloc in North America created by the governments of the United States, Canada, and Mexico. The agreement creating the trade bloc came into force on January 1, 1994. It superseded the Canada-United States Free Trade Agreement between the U.S. and Canada.

a. Collusion
b. Chief executive officer
c. North American Free Trade Agreement
d. Moving average

24. _________ is a specific term used in companies' financial reporting from the company-whole point of view. Because that use excludes the effects of changing ownership interest, an economic measure of _________ is necessary for financial analysis from the shareholders' point of view

_________ is defined by the Financial Accounting Standards Board, or FASB, as 'the change in equity [net assets] of a business enterprise during a period from transactions and other events and circumstances from nonowner sources. It includes all changes in equity during a period except those resulting from investments by owners and distributions to owners.'

_________ is the sum of net income and other items that must bypass the income statement because they have not been realized, including items like an unrealized holding gain or loss from available for sale securities and foreign currency translation gains or losses.

a. BNSF Railway
b. 3M Company
c. Comprehensive income
d. BMC Software, Inc.

25. In financial and business accounting, _________ is a measure of a firm's profitability that excludes interest and income tax expenses.

EBIT = Operating Revenue - Operating Expenses (OPEX) + Non-operating Income

Operating Income = Operating Revenue - Operating Expenses

Operating income is the difference between operating revenues and operating expenses, but it is also sometimes used as a synonym for EBIT and operating profit. This is true if the firm has no non-operating income.

a. AMEX
b. Earnings before interest and taxes
c. ABC Television Network
d. AIG

26. _________ is a fee paid on borrowed assets. It is the price paid for the use of borrowed money , or, money earned by deposited funds .Assets that are sometimes lent with _________ include money, shares, consumer goods through hire purchase, major assets such as aircraft, and even entire factories in finance lease arrangements. The _________ is calculated upon the value of the assets in the same manner as upon money.

a. Interest
b. Insolvency
c. AIG
d. ABC Television Network

27. A _________ is an annual report required by the U.S. Securities and Exchange Commission (SEC), that gives a comprehensive summary of a public company's performance. Although similarly named, the annual report on _________ is distinct from the often glossy 'annual report to shareholders', which a company must send to its shareholders when it holds an annual meeting to elect directors (though some companies combine the annual report and the 10-K into one document.) The 10-K includes information such as company history, organizational structure, executive compensation, equity, subsidiaries, and audited financial statements, among other information.

a. 3M Company
b. Form 10-Q
c. Form 10-K
d. Form 8-K

28. An _________ is a term used in behavioral economics to describe those types of behaviors that impose costs on a person in the long-run that are not taken into account when making decisions in the present. Classical Economics discourages government from creating legislation that targets internalities, because it is assumed that the consumer takes these personal costs into account when paying for the good that causes the _________. For example, cigarettes should be taxed because of the negative consumption externalities that they impose, such as second-hand smoke, not because the smoker harms him or herself by smoking.

a. Authorised capital
b. Internality
c. Operating budget
d. Inventory turnover ratio

29. _________ is concerned with the provisions and use of accounting information to managers within organizations, to provide them with the basis to make informed business decisions that will allow them to be better equipped in their management and control functions.

In contrast to financial accountancy information, _________ information is:

- usually confidential and used by management, instead of publicly reported;
- forward-looking, instead of historical;
- pragmatically computed using extensive management information systems and internal controls, instead of complying with accounting standards.

This is because of the different emphasis: _________ information is used within an organization, typically for decision-making.

a. Management accounting
b. Governmental accounting
c. Nonassurance services
d. Grenzplankostenrechnung

30. In business and accounting, _________ are everything of value that is owned by a person or company. It is a claim on the property your income of a borrower. The balance sheet of a firm records the monetary value of the _________ owned by the firm.

a. Assets
b. Accounts receivable
c. Earnings before interest, taxes, depreciation and amortization
d. Accrual basis accounting

31. _________ is the balance of the amounts of cash being received and paid by a business during a defined period of time, sometimes tied to a specific project. Measurement of _________ can be used

- to evaluate the state or performance of a business or project.
- to determine problems with liquidity. Being profitable does not necessarily mean being liquid. A company can fail because of a shortage of cash, even while profitable.
- to project rate of returns. The time of _________s into and out of projects are used as inputs to financial models such as internal rate of return, and net present value.
- to examine income or growth of a business when it is believed that accrual accounting concepts do not represent economic realities. Alternately, _________ can be used to 'validate' the net income generated by accrual accounting.

_________ as a generic term may be used differently depending on context, and certain _________ definitions may be adapted by analysts and users for their own uses. Common terms include operating _________ and free _________.

a. Flow-through entity
b. Cash Flow
c. Commercial paper
d. Controlling interest

32. In financial accounting, a _________ or Statement of cash flows is a financial statement that shows a company's flow of cash. The money coming into the business is called cash inflow, and money going out from the business is called cash outflow. The statement shows how changes in balance sheet and income accounts affect cash and cash equivalents, and breaks the analysis down to operating, investing, and financing activities.
a. BMC Software, Inc.
b. 3M Company
c. BNSF Railway
d. Cash flow statement

33. _________ is that which is owed; usually referencing assets owed, but the term can also cover moral obligations and other interactions not requiring money. In the case of assets, _________ is a means of using future purchasing power in the present before a summation has been earned. Some companies and corporations use _________ as a part of their overall corporate finance strategy.

a. Loan
b. Debenture
c. Lender
d. Debt

34. _________ is a financial ratio that indicates the percentage of a company's assets are provided via debt. It is the ratio of total debt (the sum of current liabilities and long-term liabilities) and total assets (the sum of current assets, fixed assets, and other assets such as 'goodwill'.)

$$\text{Debt ratio} = \frac{\text{Total Debt}}{\text{Total Assets}}$$

or alternatively:

$$\text{Debt ratio} = \frac{\text{Total Liability}}{\text{Total Assets}}$$

For example, a company with $2 million in total assets and $500,000 in total liabilities would have a _________ of 25%

Like all financial ratios, a company's _________ should be compared with their industry average or other competing firms.

a. 3M Company
b. Profitability index
c. Finance lease
d. Debt ratio

35. The _________ is a private, not-for-profit organization whose primary purpose is to develop generally accepted accounting principles (GAAP) within the United States in the public's interest. The Securities and Exchange Commission (SEC) designated the _________ as the organization responsible for setting accounting standards for public companies in the U.S. It was created in 1973, replacing the Accounting Principles Board and the Committee on Accounting Procedure of the American Institute of Certified Public Accountants. The _________'s mission is 'to establish and improve standards of financial accounting and reporting for the guidance and education of the public, including issuers, auditors, and users of financial information.'

The _________ is not a governmental body.

a. Public company
b. Governmental Accounting Standards Board
c. Financial Accounting Standards Board
d. Fannie Mae

36. _________ is the term used to refer to the standard framework of guidelines for financial accounting used in any given jurisdiction. _________ includes the standards, conventions, and rules accountants follow in recording and summarizing transactions, and in the preparation of financial statements.

Financial accounting information must be assembled and reported objectively.

a. General ledger
b. Current asset
c. Long-term liabilities
d. Generally accepted accounting principles

37. A _________ is a fungible, negotiable instrument representing financial value. they are broadly categorized into debt securities (such as banknotes, bonds and debentures), and equity securities; e.g., common stocks. The company or other entity issuing the _________ is called the issuer.

a. Tracking stock
b. BMC Software, Inc.
c. 3M Company
d. Security

38. The U.S. _________ is an independent agency of the United States government which holds primary responsibility for enforcing the federal securities laws and regulating the securities industry, the nation's stock and options exchanges, and other electronic securities markets. The SEC was created by section 4 of the Securities Exchange Act of 1934 (now codified as 15 U.S.C. ÂÂ§ 78d and commonly referred to as the 1934 Act.)

a. BMC Software, Inc.
b. BNSF Railway
c. 3M Company
d. Securities and Exchange Commission

39. _________ of something is, in finance, the adding together of interest or different investments over a period of time such as atoms (1 - the act or process of accruing; 2 - the amount that accrues.) It holds specific meanings in accounting and payroll.

_________, in accounting, describes the accounting method known as _________ basis, whereby revenues and expenses are recognized when they are accrued, i.e. accumulated (earned or incurred), regardless when the actual cash is received or paid out.

a. Accounts receivable
b. Earnings before interest, taxes, depreciation and amortization
c. Assets
d. Accrual

40. _________ is a method of accounting whereby economic activities (rather than cash flow) of financial events are considered, because of two complementary principles, which (together) determine the point, at which expenses and revenues are recognized. According to revenue recognition principle, revenues are realized when earned, whether or not they are received in cash.

a. Earnings before interest, taxes, depreciation and amortization
b. Accrued revenue
c. Accrual
d. Accrual basis accounting

41. _________ are the earnings returned on the initial investment amount.

In the US, the Financial Accounting Standards Board (FASB) requires companies' income statements to report _________ for each of the major categories of the income statement: continuing operations, discontinued operations, extraordinary items, and net income.

The _________ formula does not include preferred dividends for categories outside of continued operations and net income.

a. Average accounting return
b. Earnings per share
c. Earnings yield
d. Invested capital

42. An _________ is a practitioner of accountancy, which is the measurement, disclosure or provision of assurance about financial information that helps managers, investors, tax authorities and other decision makers make resource allocation decisions.

The word '_________' is derived from the French 'Compter' which took its origin from the Latin 'Computare'. The word was formerly written in English as 'Accomptant', but in process of time the word, which was always pronounced by dropping the 'p', became gradually changed both in pronunciation and in orthography to its present form.

a. AMEX
b. Accountant
c. ABC Television Network
d. AIG

43. The _________ is the national, professional association of CPAs in the United States, with more than 330,000 members, including CPAs in business and industry, public practice, government, and education; student affiliates; and international associates. It sets ethical standards for the profession and U.S. auditing standards for audits of private companies; federal, state and local governments; and non-profit organizations.

Approximately 40% of its members are engaged in the practice of public accounting, in areas such as auditing, accounting, taxation, general business consulting, business valuation, personal financial planning and business technology.

a. Other postemployment benefits
b. ABC Television Network
c. AIG
d. American Institute of Certified Public Accountants

44. _________ is the statutory title of qualified accountants in the United States who have passed the Uniform _________ Examination and have met additional state education and experience requirements for certification as a _________. Individuals who have passed the Exam but have not either accomplished the required on-the-job experience or have previously met it but in the meantime have lapsed their continuing professional education are, in many states, permitted the designation '_________ Inactive' or an equivalent phrase. In most U.S. states, only _________s who are licensed are able to provide to the public attestation (including auditing) opinions on financial statements.

a. Certified General Accountant
b. Certified Public Accountant
c. Chartered Accountant
d. Chartered Certified Accountant

45. _________ is a term used in accounting, economics and finance to spread the cost of an asset over the span of several years.

In simple words we can say that _________ is the reduction in the value of an asset due to usage, passage of time, wear and tear, technological outdating or obsolescence, depletion, inadequacy, rot, rust, decay or other such factors.

In accounting, _________ is a term used to describe any method of attributing the historical or purchase cost of an asset across its useful life, roughly corresponding to normal wear and tear.

a. Current asset
b. General ledger
c. Net profit
d. Depreciation

46. _________ are formal records of a business' financial activities.

In British English, including United Kingdom company law, _________ are often referred to as accounts, although the term _________ is also used, particularly by accountants.

_________ provide an overview of a business' financial condition in both short and long term.

a. Statement of retained earnings
b. 3M Company
c. Financial statements
d. Notes to the financial statements

47. _________ are ten auditing standards, developed by the AICPA, consisting of general standards, standards of field work, and standards of reporting, along with interpretations. They were developed by the AICPA in 1947 and have undergone minor changes since then.

The _________ are as follows:

1. The auditor must have adequate technical training and proficiency to perform the audit
2. The auditor must maintain independence in mental attitude in all matters related to the audit.
3. The auditor must use due professional care during the performance of the audit and the preparation of the report.

1. The auditor must adequately plan the work and must properly supervise any assistants.
2. The auditor must obtain a sufficient understanding of the entity and its environment, including its internal control, to assess the risk of material misstatement of the financial statements whether due to error or fraud, and to design the nature, timing, and extent of further audit procedures.
3. The auditor must obtain sufficient appropriate audit evidence by performing audit procedures to afford a reasonable basis for an opinion regarding the financial statements under audit.

The new standards are in effect for audits of financial statements for periods beginning on or after December 15, 2006.

1. The auditor must state in the auditor's report whether the financial statements are in accordance with generally accepted accounting principles (GAAP.)
2. The auditor must identify in the auditor's report those circumstances in which such principles have not been consistently observed in the current period in relation to the preceding period.
3. When the auditor determines that informative disclosures are not reasonably adequate, the auditor must so state in the auditor's report.
4. The auditor must either express an opinion regarding the financial statements, taken as a whole the auditor should state the reasons therefore in the auditor's report. In all cases where the auditor's name is associated with the financial statements, the auditor should clearly indicate the character of the auditor's work, if any, and the degree of responsibility the auditor is taking, in the auditor's report.

.

a. Continuous auditing
b. Negative assurance
c. Generally accepted auditing standards
d. Joint audit

48. _________ is a business, economics or investment term that refers to an asset's ability to be easily converted through an act of buying or selling without causing a significant movement in the price and with minimum loss of value. Money, or cash on hand, is the most liquid asset. An act of exchange of a less liquid asset with a more liquid asset is called liquidation.

a. Market liquidity
b. Financial instruments
c. Transfer agent
d. Spot rate

49. _________, commonly abbreviated as SAS, provide guidance to external auditors on generally accepted auditing standards in regards to auditing an entity and issuing a report. They are usually issued by the certified public accountant authoritative body in the region where the standards apply, such as the American Institute of Certified Public Accountants in the United States.

- _________
- _________ (Taiwan)

.

a. GASB 45
b. Financial Instruments and Exchange Law
c. RSM International
d. Statements on Auditing Standards

50. In economics, the _________, (or _________) measures the payments that flow between any individual country and all other countries. It is used to summarize all international economic transactions for that country during a specific time period, usually a year. The _________ is determined by the country's exports and imports of goods, services, and financial capital, as well as financial transfers.
a. Stock split
b. Yield to maturity
c. Moving average
d. Balance of payments

51. _________ is a method of accounting whereby cash flow of financial events is considered. The method recognizes revenues when cash is received and recognizes expenses when cash is paid out. In cash accounting, revenues and expenses are also called cash receipts and cash payments respectively.
a. Cash basis accounting
b. Closing entries
c. Treasury stock
d. Net sales

52. The _________, sometimes known as the nominal ledger, is the main accounting record of a business which uses double-entry bookkeeping. It will usually include accounts for such items as current assets, fixed assets, liabilities, revenue and expense items, gains and losses.

The _________ is a collection of the group of accounts that supports the items shown in the major financial statements.

a. Sales journal
b. General journal
c. Journal entry
d. General ledger

53. In accounting, _________ has a very specific meaning. It is an outflow of cash or other valuable assets from a person or company to another person or company. This outflow of cash is generally one side of a trade for products or services that have equal or better current or future value to the buyer than to the seller.
a. AIG
b. AMEX
c. ABC Television Network
d. Expense

54. The general definition of an _________ is an evaluation of a person, organization, system, process, project or product. _________s are performed to ascertain the validity and reliability of information; also to provide an assessment of a system's internal control. The goal of an _________ is to express an opinion on the person/organization/system (etc) in question, under evaluation based on work done on a test basis.
a. Assurance service
b. Audit
c. Audit regime
d. Institute of Chartered Accountants of India

55. A _________ has several related meanings:

- a daily record of events or business; a private _________ is usually referred to as a diary.
- a newspaper or other periodical, in the literal sense of one published each day;
- many publications issued at stated intervals, such as magazines, or scholarly academic _________s, or the record of the transactions of a society, are often called _________s. Although _________ is sometimes used, erroneously, as a synonym for 'magazine,' in academic use, a _________ refers to a serious, scholarly publication, most often peer-reviewed. A non-scholarly magazine written for an educated audience about an industry or an area of professional activity is usually called a professional magazine.

The word 'journalist' for one whose business is writing for the public press has been in use since the end of the 17th century.

Open access _________s are scholarly _________s that are available to the reader without financial or other barrier other than access to the internet itself. Some are subsidized, and some require payment on behalf of the author. Subsidized _________s are financed by an academic institution or a government information center.

a. BMC Software, Inc.
b. BNSF Railway
c. 3M Company
d. Journal

1. _________ can be regarded as an outcome of mental processes (cognitive process) leading to the selection of a course of action among several alternatives. Every _________ process produces a final choice. The output can be an action or an opinion of choice.

a. BNSF Railway
b. BMC Software, Inc.
c. 3M Company
d. Decision making

2. _________ or economic opportunity loss is the value of the next best alternative foregone as the result of making a decision. _________ analysis is an important part of a company's decision-making processes but is not treated as an actual cost in any financial statement. The next best thing that a person can engage in is referred to as the _________ of doing the best thing and ignoring the next best thing to be done.

a. Opportunity cost
b. Inflation
c. AIG
d. ABC Television Network

3. A _________ is the pinnacle activity involved in selling products or services in return for money or other compensation. It is an act of completion of a commercial activity.

A _________ is completed by the seller, the owner of the goods.

a. Tertiary sector of economy
b. Sale
c. High yield stock
d. Maturity

4. In economics, business, retail, and accounting, a _________ is the value of money that has been used up to produce something, and hence is not available for use anymore. In economics, a _________ is an alternative that is given up as a result of a decision. In business, the _________ may be one of acquisition, in which case the amount of money expended to acquire it is counted as _________.

a. Cost
b. Prime cost
c. Cost allocation
d. Cost of quality

5. _________ is a concept that denotes the precise probability of specific eventualities. Technically, the notion of _________ is independent from the notion of value and, as such, eventualities may have both beneficial and adverse consequences. However, in general usage the convention is to focus only on potential negative impact to some characteristic of value that may arise from a future event.

a. Discounting
b. Risk
c. Discount factor
d. Risk adjusted return on capital

6. _________ is a term used in subtly different ways in a number of fields, including philosophy, physics, statistics, economics, finance, insurance, psychology, sociology, engineering, and information science. It applies to predictions of future events, to physical measurements already made, or to the unknown.

In his seminal work Risk, _________, and Profit University of Chicago economist Frank Knight (1921) established the important distinction between risk and _________:

> '_________ must be taken in a sense radically distinct from the familiar notion of risk, from which it has never been properly separated....

a. ABC Television Network
b. Uncertainty
c. AMEX
d. AIG

7. An _________ is a comprehensive report on a company's activities throughout the preceding year. _________s are intended to give shareholders and other interested persons information about the company's activities and financial performance. Most jurisdictions require companies to prepare and disclose _________s, and many require the _________ to be filed at the company's registry.

a. AIG
b. ABC Television Network
c. AMEX
d. Annual Report

8. _________ is a company's financial statement that indicates how the revenue is transformed into the net income The purpose of the _________ is to show managers and investors whether the company made or lost money during the period being reported.

The important thing to remember about an _________ is that it represents a period of time.

a. ABC Television Network
b. Income Statement
c. AIG
d. AMEX

9. The _________ is one of the basic financial statements as per Generally Accepted Accounting Principles, and it explains the changes in a company's retained earnings over the reporting period. It breaks down changes affecting the account, such as profits or losses from operations, dividends paid, and any other items charged or credited to retained earnings. A retained earnings statement is required by Generally Accepted Accounting Principles whenever comparative balance sheets and income statements are presented.
a. Notes to the financial statements
b. Financial statements
c. 3M Company
d. Statement of retained earnings

10. An _________ is a term used in behavioral economics to describe those types of behaviors that impose costs on a person in the long-run that are not taken into account when making decisions in the present. Classical Economics discourages government from creating legislation that targets internalities, because it is assumed that the consumer takes these personal costs into account when paying for the good that causes the _________. For example, cigarettes should be taxed because of the negative consumption externalities that they impose, such as second-hand smoke, not because the smoker harms him or herself by smoking.
a. Operating budget
b. Authorised capital
c. Internality
d. Inventory turnover ratio

11. _________ is concerned with the provisions and use of accounting information to managers within organizations, to provide them with the basis to make informed business decisions that will allow them to be better equipped in their management and control functions.

In contrast to financial accountancy information, _________ information is:

- usually confidential and used by management, instead of publicly reported;
- forward-looking, instead of historical;
- pragmatically computed using extensive management information systems and internal controls, instead of complying with accounting standards.

This is because of the different emphasis: _________ information is used within an organization, typically for decision-making.

a. Nonassurance services
b. Governmental accounting
c. Management accounting
d. Grenzplankostenrechnung

12. In finance, _________ also known as return on investment, rate of profit or sometimes just return, is the ratio of money gained or lost on an investment relative to the amount of money invested. The amount of money gained or lost may be referred to as interest, profit/loss, gain/loss, or net income/loss. The money invested may be referred to as the asset, capital, principal, or the cost basis of the investment.
a. Theoretical ex-rights price
b. Debt to capital ratio
c. Capital employed
d. Rate of return

13. In economics, the _________, (or _________) measures the payments that flow between any individual country and all other countries. It is used to summarize all international economic transactions for that country during a specific time period, usually a year. The _________ is determined by the country's exports and imports of goods, services, and financial capital, as well as financial transfers.
a. Yield to maturity
b. Stock split
c. Moving average
d. Balance of payments

14. _________ is that which is owed; usually referencing assets owed, but the term can also cover moral obligations and other interactions not requiring money. In the case of assets, _________ is a means of using future purchasing power in the present before a summation has been earned. Some companies and corporations use _________ as a part of their overall corporate finance strategy.
a. Lender
b. Loan
c. Debenture
d. Debt

15. The _________, sometimes known as the nominal ledger, is the main accounting record of a business which uses double-entry bookkeeping. It will usually include accounts for such items as current assets, fixed assets, liabilities, revenue and expense items, gains and losses.

The _________ is a collection of the group of accounts that supports the items shown in the major financial statements.

a. Sales journal
b. General ledger
c. Journal entry
d. General journal

16. A _________ is used in research to outline possible courses of action or to present a preferred approach to an idea or thought. For example, the philosopher Isaiah Berlin used the 'hedgehogs' versus 'foxes' approach; a 'hedgehog' might approach the world in terms of a single organizing principle; a 'fox' might pursue multiple conflicting goals simultaneously. Alternatively, an empiricist might approach a subject by direct examination, whereas an intuitionist might simply intuit what's next.
a. BNSF Railway
b. 3M Company
c. BMC Software, Inc.
d. Conceptual Framework

17. A _________ is a business that functions without the intention or threat of liquidation for the foreseeable future, usually regarded as at least within 12 months.

In accounting, '_________' refers to a company's ability to continue functioning as a business entity. It is the responsibility of the directors to assess whether the _________ assumption is appropriate when preparing the financial statements.

a. BMC Software, Inc.
b. 3M Company
c. Going concern
d. Payment

18. _________ is a political and social term from the Latin verb conservare meaning to save or preserve. As the name suggests it usually indicates support for tradition and traditional values though the meaning has changed in different countries and time periods. The modern political term conservative was used by French politician Chateaubriand in 1819.
a. 3M Company
b. Politicized issue
c. Conservatism
d. BMC Software, Inc.

19. The _________ is a private, not-for-profit organization whose primary purpose is to develop generally accepted accounting principles (GAAP) within the United States in the public's interest. The Securities and Exchange Commission (SEC) designated the _________ as the organization responsible for setting accounting standards for public companies in the U.S. It was created in 1973, replacing the Accounting Principles Board and the Committee on Accounting Procedure of the American Institute of Certified Public Accountants. The _________'s mission is 'to establish and improve standards of financial accounting and reporting for the guidance and education of the public, including issuers, auditors, and users of financial information.'

The _________ is not a governmental body.

a. Fannie Mae
b. Governmental Accounting Standards Board
c. Public company
d. Financial Accounting Standards Board

20. _________ describes the situation when output from (or information about the result of) an event or phenomenon in the past will influence the same event/phenomenon in the present or future. When an event is part of a chain of cause-and-effect that forms a circuit or loop, then the event is said to 'feed back' into itself.

_________ is also a synonym for:

- _________ Signal; the information about the initial event that is the basis for subsequent modification of the event.
- _________ Loop; the causal path that leads from the initial generation of the _________ signal to the subsequent modification of the event.

_________ is a mechanism, process or signal that is looped back to control a system within itself. Such a loop is called a _________ loop.

a. BMC Software, Inc.
b. 3M Company
c. Controllable
d. Feedback

21. A _________ is a fungible, negotiable instrument representing financial value. they are broadly categorized into debt securities (such as banknotes, bonds and debentures), and equity securities; e.g., common stocks. The company or other entity issuing the _________ is called the issuer.

a. BMC Software, Inc.
b. Tracking stock
c. Security
d. 3M Company

22. The U.S. _________ is an independent agency of the United States government which holds primary responsibility for enforcing the federal securities laws and regulating the securities industry, the nation's stock and options exchanges, and other electronic securities markets. The SEC was created by section 4 of the Securities Exchange Act of 1934 (now codified as 15 U.S.C. ÂÂ§ 78d and commonly referred to as the 1934 Act.)
a. BMC Software, Inc.
b. 3M Company
c. BNSF Railway
d. Securities and Exchange Commission

23. In mathematics, two elements x and y of a set partially ordered by a relation ≤ are said to be _________ if and only if x ≤ y or y ≤ x if and only if x < y or y < x or y = x. For example, two sets are _________ with respect to inclusion if and only if one is a subset of the other.

In a classification of mathematical objects such as topological spaces, two criteria are said to be _________ when the objects that obey one criterion constitute a subset of the objects that obey the other one .

a. Scientific Research and Experimental Development Tax Incentive Program
b. Database auditing
c. Consumption
d. Comparable

24. A _________ proof is a mathematical proof that a particular theory is consistent. The early development of mathematical proof theory was driven by the desire to provide finitary _________ proofs for all of mathematics as part of Hilbert's program. Hilbert's program was strongly impacted by incompleteness theorems, which showed that sufficiently strong proof theories cannot prove their own _________
a. Consistency
b. Monte Carlo methods
c. Daybook
d. Consumption

25. In financial accounting, a _________ or statement of financial position is a summary of a person's or organization's balances. Assets, liabilities and ownership equity are listed as of a specific date, such as the end of its financial year. A _________ is often described as a snapshot of a company's financial condition.

a. Financial statements
b. Statement of retained earnings
c. 3M Company
d. Balance Sheet

1. An _________ is a comprehensive report on a company's activities throughout the preceding year. _________s are intended to give shareholders and other interested persons information about the company's activities and financial performance. Most jurisdictions require companies to prepare and disclose _________s, and many require the _________ to be filed at the company's registry.

a. ABC Television Network
b. AIG
c. AMEX
d. Annual Report

2. In financial accounting, a _________ or statement of financial position is a summary of a person's or organization's balances. Assets, liabilities and ownership equity are listed as of a specific date, such as the end of its financial year. A _________ is often described as a snapshot of a company's financial condition.

a. Statement of retained earnings
b. Financial statements
c. Balance Sheet
d. 3M Company

3. _________ is that which is owed; usually referencing assets owed, but the term can also cover moral obligations and other interactions not requiring money. In the case of assets, _________ is a means of using future purchasing power in the present before a summation has been earned. Some companies and corporations use _________ as a part of their overall corporate finance strategy.

a. Debt
b. Lender
c. Debenture
d. Loan

4. The _________ is a private, not-for-profit organization whose primary purpose is to develop generally accepted accounting principles (GAAP) within the United States in the public's interest. The Securities and Exchange Commission (SEC) designated the _________ as the organization responsible for setting accounting standards for public companies in the U.S. It was created in 1973, replacing the Accounting Principles Board and the Committee on Accounting Procedure of the American Institute of Certified Public Accountants. The _________'s mission is 'to establish and improve standards of financial accounting and reporting for the guidance and education of the public, including issuers, auditors, and users of financial information.'

The _________ is not a governmental body.

a. Governmental Accounting Standards Board
b. Public company
c. Fannie Mae
d. Financial Accounting Standards Board

5. An _________ is a term used in behavioral economics to describe those types of behaviors that impose costs on a person in the long-run that are not taken into account when making decisions in the present. Classical Economics discourages government from creating legislation that targets internalities, because it is assumed that the consumer takes these personal costs into account when paying for the good that causes the _________. For example, cigarettes should be taxed because of the negative consumption externalities that they impose, such as second-hand smoke, not because the smoker harms him or herself by smoking.
a. Authorised capital
b. Inventory turnover ratio
c. Operating budget
d. Internality

6. In economics, _________ or _________ goods or real _________ refers to factors of production used to create goods or services that are not themselves significantly consumed (though they may depreciate) in the production process. _________ goods may be acquired with money or financial _________. In finance and accounting, _________ generally refers to financial wealth, especially that used to start or maintain a business.
a. Capital
b. Vyborg Appeal
c. Screening
d. Disclosure

7. In finance, _________ refers to the way a corporation finances its assets through some combination of equity, debt, or hybrid securities. A firm's _________ is then the composition or 'structure' of its liabilities. For example, a firm that sells $20 billion in equity and $80 billion in debt is said to be 20% equity-financed and 80% debt-financed.
a. Restricted stock
b. Flow-through entity
c. Gross income
d. Capital structure

8. _________ and credit are formal bookkeeping and accounting terms. They are the most fundamental concepts in accounting, representing the two records that one party in a transaction makes on its records, transferring a money balance from one account to another, one representing a reduction of liability or increase in asset, and the other representing a balancing increase in liability or reduction of asset.

Introduction

_________s and credits are a system of notation used in accounting to keep track of money movements (transactions) into and out of an account.

a. Debit and credit
b. Bookkeeping
c. Debit
d. Cookie jar accounting

9. In financial accounting, a _________ is defined as an obligation of an entity arising from past transactions or events, the settlement of which may result in the transfer or use of assets, provision of services or other yielding of economic benefits in the future.
a. Vested
b. Corporate governance
c. False Claims Act
d. Liability

10. In business and accounting, _________ are everything of value that is owned by a person or company. It is a claim on the property your income of a borrower. The balance sheet of a firm records the monetary value of the _________ owned by the firm.
a. Accrual basis accounting
b. Assets
c. Accounts receivable
d. Earnings before interest, taxes, depreciation and amortization

11. _________ is the state or fact of exclusive rights and control over property, which may be an object, land/real estate or intellectual property. An _________ right is also referred to as title.

_________ is the key building block in the development of the capitalist socio-economic system.

a. Ownership
b. Administrative proceeding
c. Encumbrance
d. ABC Television Network

12. A sole _________, or simply _________ is a type of business entity which legally has no separate existence from its owner. Hence, the limitations of liability enjoyed by a corporation and limited liability partnerships do not apply to sole proprietors. All debts of the business are debts of the owner.

a. Proprietorship
b. Pre-determined overhead rate
c. Free cash flow
d. Safety stock

13. The _________ are the primary rules governing the management of a corporation in the United States and Canada, and are filed with a state or other regulatory agency. The equivalent in the United Kingdom and various other countries is Articles of Association.

A corporation's _________ generally provide information such as:

- The corporation's name, which has to be unique from any other corporation in that jurisdiction. As part of the corporation's name, certain words such as 'incorporated', 'limited', 'corporation', (or their abbreviations) or some equivalent term in countries whose language is not English, are usually required as part of the name as a 'flag' to indicate to persons doing business with the organization that it is a corporation as opposed to an individual or partnership (with unlimited liability.) In some cases, certain types of names are prohibited except by special permission, such as words implying the corporation is a government agency or has powers to act in ways it is not otherwise allowed.
- The name of the person(s) organizing the corporation (usually members of the board of directors.)
- Whether the corporation is a stock corporation or a non-stock corporation.
- Whether the corporation's existence is permanent or limited for a specific period of time. Generally the rule is that a corporation existence is forever, or until (1) it stops paying the yearly corporate renewal fees or otherwise fails to do something required to continue its existence such as file certain paperwork each year; or (2) it files a request to 'wind up and dissolve.'
- In some cases, a corporation must state the purposes for which it is formed. Some jurisdictions permit a general statement such as 'any lawful purpose' but some require explicit specifications.
- If a non-stock corporation, whether it is for profit or non-profit. However, some jurisdictions differentiate by 'for profit' or 'non profit' and some by 'stock or non-stock'.
- In the United States, if a corporation is to be organized as a non-profit, to be recognized as such by the Internal Revenue Service, such as for eligibility for tax exemption, certain specific wording must be included stating no part of the assets of the corporation are to benefit the members.
- If a stock corporation, the number of shares the corporation is authorized to issue, or the maximum amount in a specific currency of stock that may be issued, e.g. a maximum of $25,000.
- The number and names of the corporation's initial Board of Directors (though this is optional in most cases.)
- The initial director(s) of the corporation (in some cases the incorporator or the registered agent must be a director, if not an attorney or another corporation.)
- The location of the corporation's 'registered office' - the location at which legal papers can be served to the corporation if necessary. Some states further require the designation of a Registered Agent: a person to whom such papers could be delivered.

Most states permit a corporation to be formed by one person; in some cases (such as non-profit corporations) it may require three or five or more. This change has come about as a result of Delaware liberalizing its corporation rules to allow corporations to be formed by one person, and states not wanting to lose corporate charters to Delaware had to revise their rules as a result.

a. Exclusive right
b. Express warranty
c. Articles of incorporation
d. Employee Retirement Income Security Act

14. A _________ is a body of elected or appointed members who jointly oversee the activities of a company or organization. The body sometimes has a different name, such as board of trustees, board of governors, board of managers, or executive board. It is often simply referred to as 'the board.'

A board's activities are determined by the powers, duties, and responsibilities delegated to it or conferred on it by an authority outside itself.

a. Hospital Survey and Construction Act
b. Consumer protection laws
c. Chief Financial Officers Act of 1990
d. Board of directors

15. _________ can refer to a law of local or limited application, passed under the authority of a higher law specifying what things may be regulated by the _________, or it can refer to the internal rules of a company or organisation.
a. Bylaw
b. Scottish Poor Laws
c. Letter of credit
d. Lease

16. _________ is a company's financial statement that indicates how the revenue is transformed into the net income The purpose of the _________ is to show managers and investors whether the company made or lost money during the period being reported.

The important thing to remember about an _________ is that it represents a period of time.

a. ABC Television Network
b. AIG
c. AMEX
d. Income Statement

17. An _________ is a mostly hierarchical concept of subordination of entities that collaborate and contribute to serve one common aim.

Organizations are a variant of clustered entities. The structure of an organization is usually set up in many a styles, dependent on their objectives and ambience.

a. AMEX
b. AIG
c. ABC Television Network
d. Organizational structure

18. A _________ is a type of business entity in which partners (owners) share with each other the profits or losses of the business undertaking in which all have invested. _________s are often favored over corporations for taxation purposes, as the _________ structure does not generally incur a tax on profits before it is distributed to the partners (i.e. there is no dividend tax levied.) However, depending on the _________ structure and the jurisdiction in which it operates, owners of a _________ may be exposed to greater personal liability than they would as shareholders of a corporation.
a. National Information Infrastructure Protection Act
b. Resource Conservation and Recovery Act
c. Corporate governance
d. Partnership

19. _________ is the maximum number of shares that a company can issue. This number is specified in the company's articles of association but can be changed by shareholder approval. A company usually authorizes a higher number of shares than required to be able to issue stock in the future.
a. Restructuring
b. Shares authorized
c. Disposal tax effect
d. Fair market value

20. _________ is a form of corporation equity ownership represented in the securities. It is a stock whose dividends are based on market fluctuations. It is dangerous in comparison to preferred shares and some other investment options, in that in the event of bankruptcy, _________ investors receive their funds after preferred stock holders, bondholders, creditors, etc. On the other hand, common shares on average perform better than preferred shares or bonds over time.
a. 3M Company
b. Stock split
c. Growth investing
d. Common stock

21. _________ are payments made by a corporation to its shareholder members. It is the portion of corporate profits paid out to stockholders. When a corporation earns a profit or surplus, that money can be put to two uses: it can either be re-invested in the business (called retained earnings), or it can be paid to the shareholders as a dividend.

a. Dividend payout ratio
b. Dividend yield
c. Dividend stripping
d. Dividends

22. _________ is a term of law and finance for the quantity of shares of a corporation, which have been sold or awarded and are subsequently held by the shareholders.

The number of _________ usually a subset of the total authorized shares, which the board of directors and/or shareholders have agreed to distribute under certain circumstances.

- Shares authorized = Shares issued + Shares unissued
- Shares issued = Shares outstanding + Treasury stock

.

a. Operating Lease
b. Exclusive right
c. Issued shares
d. Investment Advisers Act of 1940

23. _________ are common shares that have been authorized, issued, and purchased by investors. They have voting rights and represent ownership in the corporation by the person or institution that holds the shares. They should be distinguished from treasury shares, which are common stock repurchased by the corporation.
a. Controlling interest
b. Shares outstanding
c. Preferred stock
d. Participating preferred stock

24. A _________ or reacquired stock is stock which is bought back by the issuing company, reducing the amount of outstanding stock on the open market ('open market' including insiders' holdings).

Stock repurchases are often used as a tax-efficient method to put cash into shareholders' hands, rather than pay dividends. Sometimes, companies do this when they feel that their stock is undervalued on the open market.

a. Matching principle
b. Treasury stock
c. Cost of goods sold
d. Net profit

25. _________, in finance and accounting, means stated value or face value. From this comes the expressions at par (at the _________), over par (over _________) and under par (under _________).

_________ is a nominal value of a security which is determined by an issuer company at a minimum price. _________ of an equity (a stock) is a somewhat archaic concept. The _________ of a stock was the share price upon initial offering; the issuing company promised not to issue further shares below _________, so investors could be confident that no one else was receiving a more favorable issue price. This was far more important in unregulated equity markets than in the regulated markets that exist today.

a. Par value
b. Creditor
c. Restructuring
d. Net worth

26. _________ is typically a 'higher ranking' stock than voting shares, and its terms are negotiated between the corporation and the investor.

_________ usually carries no voting rights, but may carry superior priority over common stock in the payment of dividends and upon liquidation. _________ may carry a dividend that is paid out prior to any dividends being paid to common stock holders.

a. Restricted stock
b. Gross income
c. Preferred stock
d. Cash flow

27. A _________ is the transfer of an interest in property (or the equivalent in law - a charge) to a lender as a security for a debt - usually a loan of money. While a _________ in itself is not a debt, it is the lender's security for a debt. It is a transfer of an interest in land (or the equivalent) from the owner to the _________ lender, on the condition that this interest will be returned to the owner when the terms of the _________ have been satisfied or performed.

a. BMC Software, Inc.
b. Mortgage
c. BNSF Railway
d. 3M Company

28. A _________, also referred to as a note payable in accounting, is a contract where one party (the maker or issuer) makes an unconditional promise in writing to pay a sum of money to the other (the payee), either at a fixed or determinable future time or on demand of the payee, under specific terms. They differ from IOUs in that they contain a specific promise to pay, rather than simply acknowledging that a debt exists.

The terms of a note typically include the principal amount, the interest rate if any, and the maturity date.

a. 3M Company
b. BMC Software, Inc.
c. BNSF Railway
d. Promissory note

29. In economics, business, retail, and accounting, a _________ is the value of money that has been used up to produce something, and hence is not available for use anymore. In economics, a _________ is an alternative that is given up as a result of a decision. In business, the _________ may be one of acquisition, in which case the amount of money expended to acquire it is counted as _________.
a. Prime cost
b. Cost of quality
c. Cost allocation
d. Cost

30. A _________ is a type of debt Like all debt instruments, a _________ entails the redistribution of financial assets over time, between the lender and the borrower.
a. Loan
b. Debenture
c. Loan to value
d. Lender

31. In finance, a _________ is a debt security, in which the authorized issuer owes the holders a debt and, depending on the terms of the _________, is obliged to pay interest (the coupon) and/or to repay the principal at a later date, termed maturity. It is a formal contract to repay borrowed money with interest at fixed intervals.

Thus a _________ is like a loan: the issuer is the borrower, the _________ holder is the lender, and the coupon is the interest.

a. Coupon rate
b. Revenue bonds
c. Zero-coupon bond
d. Bond

32. The _________ is a financial market where participants buy and sell debt securities, usually in the form of bonds. As of 2006, the size of the international _________ is an estimated $44.9 trillion, of which the size of the outstanding U.S. _________ debt was $25.2 trillion.

Nearly all of the $923 billion average daily trading volume in the U.S. _________ takes place between broker-dealers and large institutions in a decentralized, over-the-counter market.

a. Demand curve
b. Variance
c. Bond Market
d. Convertible bond

33. A _________ is defined as a certificate of agreement of loans which is given under the company's stamp and carries an undertaking that the _________ holder will get a fixed return (fixed on the basis of interest rates) and the principal amount whenever the _________ matures.

In finance, a _________ is a long-term debt instrument used by governments and large companies to obtain funds. It is defined as 'any form of borrowing that commits a firm to pay interest and repay capital.

a. Loan
b. Credit rating
c. Loan to value
d. Debenture

34. _________ is a fee paid on borrowed assets. It is the price paid for the use of borrowed money , or, money earned by deposited funds .Assets that are sometimes lent with _________ include money, shares, consumer goods through hire purchase, major assets such as aircraft, and even entire factories in finance lease arrangements. The _________ is calculated upon the value of the assets in the same manner as upon money.

a. AIG
b. ABC Television Network
c. Insolvency
d. Interest

35. A _________ is any one of a variety of different systems, institutions, procedures, social relations and infrastructures whereby persons trade, and goods and services are exchanged, forming part of the economy. It is an arrangement that allows buyers and sellers to exchange things. _________s vary in size, range, geographic scale, location, types and variety of human communities, as well as the types of goods and services traded.

a. Market Failure
b. Market
c. Recession
d. Perfect competition

36. _________ is an economic concept with commonplace familiarity. It is the price that a good or service is offered at, or will fetch, in the marketplace. It is of interest mainly in the study of microeconomics.
a. Transfer agent
b. Market price
c. Financial instruments
d. Spot rate

37. In finance and economics _________ or nominal rate of interest refers to the rate of interest before adjustment for inflation (in contrast with the real interest rate); or, for interest rates 'as stated' without adjustment for the full effect of compounding (also referred to as the nominal annual rate.) An interest rate is called nominal if the frequency of compounding (e.g. a month) is not identical to the basic time unit (normally a year.)

The real interest rate includes compensation for the lender's lost value due to inflation, whereas the _________ excludes inflation.

a. BNSF Railway
b. BMC Software, Inc.
c. 3M Company
d. Nominal interest rate

38. _________ of something is, in finance, the adding together of interest or different investments over a period of time such as atoms (1 - the act or process of accruing; 2 - the amount that accrues.) It holds specific meanings in accounting and payroll.

_________, in accounting, describes the accounting method known as _________ basis, whereby revenues and expenses are recognized when they are accrued, i.e. accumulated (earned or incurred), regardless when the actual cash is received or paid out.

a. Accounts receivable
b. Accrual
c. Earnings before interest, taxes, depreciation and amortization
d. Assets

39. _________ is a method of accounting whereby economic activities (rather than cash flow) of financial events are considered, because of two complementary principles, which (together) determine the point, at which expenses and revenues are recognized. According to revenue recognition principle, revenues are realized when earned, whether or not they are received in cash.

a. Earnings before interest, taxes, depreciation and amortization
b. Accrued revenue
c. Accrual basis accounting
d. Accrual

40. An _________ is the price a borrower pays for the use of money they do not own, for instance a small company might borrow from a bank to kick start their business, and the return a lender receives for deferring the use of funds, by lending it to the borrower. _________s are normally expressed as a percentage rate over the period of one year.

_________s targets are also a vital tool of monetary policy and are used to control variables like investment, inflation, and unemployment.

a. AIG
b. ABC Television Network
c. AMEX
d. Interest rate

41. _________ in economics and business is the result of an exchange and from that trade we assign a numerical monetary value to a good, service or asset. If Alice trades Bob 4 apples for an orange, the _________ of an orange is 4 apples. Inversely, the _________ of an apple is 1/4 oranges.

a. Price discrimination
b. Transactional Net Margin Method
c. Price
d. Discounts and allowances

42. Discounting is a financial mechanism in which a debtor obtains the right to delay payments to a creditor, for a defined period of time, in exchange for a charge or fee. Essentially, the party that owes money in the present purchases the right to delay the payment until some future date. The _________, or charge, is simply the difference between the original amount owed in the present and the amount that has to be paid in the future to settle the debt.

a. Risk aversion
b. Discount factor
c. Discounting
d. Discount

43. In economics, the _________, (or _________) measures the payments that flow between any individual country and all other countries. It is used to summarize all international economic transactions for that country during a specific time period, usually a year. The _________ is determined by the country's exports and imports of goods, services, and financial capital, as well as financial transfers.

a. Yield to maturity
b. Moving average
c. Stock split
d. Balance of payments

44. The _________, sometimes known as the nominal ledger, is the main accounting record of a business which uses double-entry bookkeeping. It will usually include accounts for such items as current assets, fixed assets, liabilities, revenue and expense items, gains and losses.

The _________ is a collection of the group of accounts that supports the items shown in the major financial statements.

a. Journal entry
b. General journal
c. Sales journal
d. General ledger

45. _________ is the balance of the amounts of cash being received and paid by a business during a defined period of time, sometimes tied to a specific project. Measurement of _________ can be used

- to evaluate the state or performance of a business or project.
- to determine problems with liquidity. Being profitable does not necessarily mean being liquid. A company can fail because of a shortage of cash, even while profitable.
- to project rate of returns. The time of _________s into and out of projects are used as inputs to financial models such as internal rate of return, and net present value.
- to examine income or growth of a business when it is believed that accrual accounting concepts do not represent economic realities. Alternately, _________ can be used to 'validate' the net income generated by accrual accounting.

_________ as a generic term may be used differently depending on context, and certain _________ definitions may be adapted by analysts and users for their own uses. Common terms include operating _________ and free _________.

a. Commercial paper
b. Controlling interest
c. Flow-through entity
d. Cash Flow

46. In financial accounting, a _________ or Statement of cash flows is a financial statement that shows a company's flow of cash. The money coming into the business is called cash inflow, and money going out from the business is called cash outflow. The statement shows how changes in balance sheet and income accounts affect cash and cash equivalents, and breaks the analysis down to operating, investing, and financing activities.

a. 3M Company
b. Cash flow statement
c. BNSF Railway
d. BMC Software, Inc.

47. _________ is a financial ratio that indicates the percentage of a company's assets are provided via debt. It is the ratio of total debt (the sum of current liabilities and long-term liabilities) and total assets (the sum of current assets, fixed assets, and other assets such as 'goodwill'.)

$$\text{Debt ratio} = \frac{\text{Total Debt}}{\text{Total Assets}}$$

or alternatively:

$$\text{Debt ratio} = \frac{\text{Total Liability}}{\text{Total Assets}}$$

For example, a company with $2 million in total assets and $500,000 in total liabilities would have a _________ of 25%

Like all financial ratios, a company's _________ should be compared with their industry average or other competing firms.

a. Finance lease
b. 3M Company
c. Profitability index
d. Debt ratio

1. An _________ is a comprehensive report on a company's activities throughout the preceding year. _________s are intended to give shareholders and other interested persons information about the company's activities and financial performance. Most jurisdictions require companies to prepare and disclose _________s, and many require the _________ to be filed at the company's registry.

a. AIG
b. ABC Television Network
c. AMEX
d. Annual Report

2. The _________ is a private, not-for-profit organization whose primary purpose is to develop generally accepted accounting principles (GAAP) within the United States in the public's interest. The Securities and Exchange Commission (SEC) designated the _________ as the organization responsible for setting accounting standards for public companies in the U.S. It was created in 1973, replacing the Accounting Principles Board and the Committee on Accounting Procedure of the American Institute of Certified Public Accountants. The _________'s mission is 'to establish and improve standards of financial accounting and reporting for the guidance and education of the public, including issuers, auditors, and users of financial information.'

The _________ is not a governmental body.

a. Fannie Mae
b. Public company
c. Governmental Accounting Standards Board
d. Financial Accounting Standards Board

3. _________ is a company's financial statement that indicates how the revenue is transformed into the net income The purpose of the _________ is to show managers and investors whether the company made or lost money during the period being reported.

The important thing to remember about an _________ is that it represents a period of time.

a. AMEX
b. Income Statement
c. ABC Television Network
d. AIG

4. _________ is a method of accounting whereby cash flow of financial events is considered. The method recognizes revenues when cash is received and recognizes expenses when cash is paid out. In cash accounting, revenues and expenses are also called cash receipts and cash payments respectively.

a. Treasury stock
b. Closing entries
c. Cash basis accounting
d. Net sales

5. In accounting, _________ has a very specific meaning. It is an outflow of cash or other valuable assets from a person or company to another person or company. This outflow of cash is generally one side of a trade for products or services that have equal or better current or future value to the buyer than to the seller.

a. AIG
b. ABC Television Network
c. AMEX
d. Expense

6. _________ is equal to the income that a firm has after subtracting costs and expenses from the total revenue. _________ can be distributed among holders of common stock as a dividend or held by the firm as retained earnings.

The items deducted will typically include tax expense, financing expense (interest expense), and minority interest. Likewise, preferred stock dividends will be subtracted too, though they are not an expense.

a. Matching principle
b. Generally accepted accounting principles
c. Long-term liabilities
d. Net income

7. _________ is a term used in accounting, economics and finance to spread the cost of an asset over the span of several years.

In simple words we can say that _________ is the reduction in the value of an asset due to usage, passage of time, wear and tear, technological outdating or obsolescence, depletion, inadequacy, rot, rust, decay or other such factors.

In accounting, _________ is a term used to describe any method of attributing the historical or purchase cost of an asset across its useful life, roughly corresponding to normal wear and tear.

a. Current asset
b. Net profit
c. General ledger
d. Depreciation

8. The term _________, derived from the distinctive T shape, is frequently used when discussing or analyzing accounting or business transactions. _________s are used to represent general ledger accounts.

Typically one or more Ts are drawn on a white board or blank piece of paper. A general ledger account name or number is then written above each T. Debit entries are recorded on the left side of the 'T' and credit entries are recorded on the right side of the 'T'.

a. 3M Company
b. BMC Software, Inc.
c. BNSF Railway
d. T account

9. _________ are formal records of a business' financial activities.

In British English, including United Kingdom company law, _________ are often referred to as accounts, although the term _________ is also used, particularly by accountants.

_________ provide an overview of a business' financial condition in both short and long term.

a. Notes to the financial statements
b. Statement of retained earnings
c. 3M Company
d. Financial statements

10. _________ of something is, in finance, the adding together of interest or different investments over a period of time such as atoms (1 - the act or process of accruing; 2 - the amount that accrues.) It holds specific meanings in accounting and payroll.

_________, in accounting, describes the accounting method known as _________ basis, whereby revenues and expenses are recognized when they are accrued, i.e. accumulated (earned or incurred), regardless when the actual cash is received or paid out.

a. Assets
b. Accounts receivable
c. Accrual
d. Earnings before interest, taxes, depreciation and amortization

11. _________ is a method of accounting whereby economic activities (rather than cash flow) of financial events are considered, because of two complementary principles, which (together) determine the point, at which expenses and revenues are recognized. According to revenue recognition principle, revenues are realized when earned, whether or not they are received in cash.

a. Earnings before interest, taxes, depreciation and amortization
b. Accrual basis accounting
c. Accrued revenue
d. Accrual

12. In economics, business, retail, and accounting, a _________ is the value of money that has been used up to produce something, and hence is not available for use anymore. In economics, a _________ is an alternative that is given up as a result of a decision. In business, the _________ may be one of acquisition, in which case the amount of money expended to acquire it is counted as _________.

a. Cost of quality
b. Prime cost
c. Cost allocation
d. Cost

13. In financial accounting, _________ or cost of sales includes the direct costs attributable to the production of the goods sold by a company. This amount includes the materials cost used in creating the goods along with the direct labor costs used to produce the good. It excludes indirect expenses such as distribution costs and sales force costs.

a. 3M Company
b. FIFO and LIFO accounting
c. Reorder point
d. Cost of goods sold

14. _________, Gross profit margin or Gross Profit Rate can be defined as the amount of contribution to the business enterprise, after paying for direct-fixed and direct-variable unit costs, required to cover overheads (fixed commitments) and provide a buffer for unknown items. It expresses the relationship between gross profit and sales revenue.

It can be expressed in absolute terms:

Gross Profit = Revenue − Cost of Goods Sold

or as the ratio of gross profit to sales revenue, usually in the form of a percentage:

_________ Percentage = (Revenue-Cost of Goods Sold)/Revenue

Cost of goods sold includes variable costs and fixed costs directly linked to the product, such as material and labor.

a. BNSF Railway
b. BMC Software, Inc.
c. 3M Company
d. Gross margin

15. _________ is the difference between operating revenues and operating expenses, but it is also sometimes used as a synonym for EBIT and operating profit. This is true if the firm has no non-_________.

A professional investor contemplating a change to the capital structure of a firm first evaluates a firm's fundamental earnings potential (reflected by Earnings Before Interest, Taxes, Depreciation and Amortization EBITDA and EBIT), and then determines the optimal use of debt vs. equity.

a. ABC Television Network
b. Operating income
c. AIG
d. AMEX

16. A _________ is the pinnacle activity involved in selling products or services in return for money or other compensation. It is an act of completion of a commercial activity.

A _________ is completed by the seller, the owner of the goods.

a. Sale
b. Maturity
c. Tertiary sector of economy
d. High yield stock

17. In financial accounting, a _________ or statement of financial position is a summary of a person's or organization's balances. Assets, liabilities and ownership equity are listed as of a specific date, such as the end of its financial year. A _________ is often described as a snapshot of a company's financial condition.

a. Financial statements
b. Balance Sheet
c. 3M Company
d. Statement of retained earnings

18. In economics, _________ or _________ goods or real _________ refers to factors of production used to create goods or services that are not themselves significantly consumed (though they may depreciate) in the production process. _________ goods may be acquired with money or financial _________. In finance and accounting, _________ generally refers to financial wealth, especially that used to start or maintain a business.

a. Vyborg Appeal
b. Disclosure
c. Screening
d. Capital

19. In finance, _________ refers to the way a corporation finances its assets through some combination of equity, debt, or hybrid securities. A firm's _________ is then the composition or 'structure' of its liabilities. For example, a firm that sells $20 billion in equity and $80 billion in debt is said to be 20% equity-financed and 80% debt-financed.

a. Restricted stock
b. Flow-through entity
c. Gross income
d. Capital structure

20. _________ and credit are formal bookkeeping and accounting terms. They are the most fundamental concepts in accounting, representing the two records that one party in a transaction makes on its records, transferring a money balance from one account to another, one representing a reduction of liability or increase in asset, and the other representing a balancing increase in liability or reduction of asset.

Introduction

_________s and credits are a system of notation used in accounting to keep track of money movements (transactions) into and out of an account.

a. Debit
b. Bookkeeping
c. Cookie jar accounting
d. Debit and credit

21. _________ is the state or fact of exclusive rights and control over property, which may be an object, land/real estate or intellectual property. An _________ right is also referred to as title.

_________ is the key building block in the development of the capitalist socio-economic system.

a. Ownership
b. ABC Television Network
c. Encumbrance
d. Administrative proceeding

22. A _________ is a body of elected or appointed members who jointly oversee the activities of a company or organization. The body sometimes has a different name, such as board of trustees, board of governors, board of managers, or executive board. It is often simply referred to as 'the board.'

A board's activities are determined by the powers, duties, and responsibilities delegated to it or conferred on it by an authority outside itself.

a. Hospital Survey and Construction Act
b. Chief Financial Officers Act of 1990
c. Consumer protection laws
d. Board of directors

23. _________ is a form of corporation equity ownership represented in the securities. It is a stock whose dividends are based on market fluctuations. It is dangerous in comparison to preferred shares and some other investment options, in that in the event of bankruptcy, _________ investors receive their funds after preferred stock holders, bondholders, creditors, etc. On the other hand, common shares on average perform better than preferred shares or bonds over time.
a. 3M Company
b. Stock split
c. Growth investing
d. Common stock

24. _________ are payments made by a corporation to its shareholder members. It is the portion of corporate profits paid out to stockholders. When a corporation earns a profit or surplus, that money can be put to two uses: it can either be re-invested in the business (called retained earnings), or it can be paid to the shareholders as a dividend.
a. Dividend payout ratio
b. Dividend stripping
c. Dividend yield
d. Dividends

25. In economics, the _________, (or _________) measures the payments that flow between any individual country and all other countries. It is used to summarize all international economic transactions for that country during a specific time period, usually a year. The _________ is determined by the country's exports and imports of goods, services, and financial capital, as well as financial transfers.

a. Stock split
b. Yield to maturity
c. Moving average
d. Balance of payments

26. _________ is a specific term used in companies' financial reporting from the company-whole point of view. Because that use excludes the effects of changing ownership interest, an economic measure of _________ is necessary for financial analysis from the shareholders' point of view

_________ is defined by the Financial Accounting Standards Board, or FASB, as 'the change in equity [net assets] of a business enterprise during a period from transactions and other events and circumstances from nonowner sources. It includes all changes in equity during a period except those resulting from investments by owners and distributions to owners.'

_________ is the sum of net income and other items that must bypass the income statement because they have not been realized, including items like an unrealized holding gain or loss from available for sale securities and foreign currency translation gains or losses.

a. BMC Software, Inc.
b. 3M Company
c. BNSF Railway
d. Comprehensive income

27. The _________, sometimes known as the nominal ledger, is the main accounting record of a business which uses double-entry bookkeeping. It will usually include accounts for such items as current assets, fixed assets, liabilities, revenue and expense items, gains and losses.

The _________ is a collection of the group of accounts that supports the items shown in the major financial statements.

a. Sales journal
b. General ledger
c. Journal entry
d. General journal

28. A _________ is the transfer of wealth from one party (such as a person or company) to another. A _________ is usually made in exchange for the provision of goods, services or both, or to fulfill a legal obligation.

The simplest and oldest form of _________ is barter, the exchange of one good or service for another.

a. 3M Company
b. BMC Software, Inc.
c. Payment
d. Payee

29. _________ is typically a 'higher ranking' stock than voting shares, and its terms are negotiated between the corporation and the investor.

_________ usually carries no voting rights, but may carry superior priority over common stock in the payment of dividends and upon liquidation. _________ may carry a dividend that is paid out prior to any dividends being paid to common stock holders.

a. Gross income
b. Restricted stock
c. Cash flow
d. Preferred stock

30. A sole _________, or simply _________ is a type of business entity which legally has no separate existence from its owner. Hence, the limitations of liability enjoyed by a corporation and limited liability partnerships do not apply to sole proprietors. All debts of the business are debts of the owner.
a. Proprietorship
b. Safety stock
c. Free cash flow
d. Pre-determined overhead rate

31. A _________ is a type of business entity in which partners (owners) share with each other the profits or losses of the business undertaking in which all have invested. _________s are often favored over corporations for taxation purposes, as the _________ structure does not generally incur a tax on profits before it is distributed to the partners (i.e. there is no dividend tax levied.) However, depending on the _________ structure and the jurisdiction in which it operates, owners of a _________ may be exposed to greater personal liability than they would as shareholders of a corporation.
a. Corporate governance
b. Partnership
c. Resource Conservation and Recovery Act
d. National Information Infrastructure Protection Act

32. The _________ is one of the basic financial statements as per Generally Accepted Accounting Principles, and it explains the changes in a company's retained earnings over the reporting period. It breaks down changes affecting the account, such as profits or losses from operations, dividends paid, and any other items charged or credited to retained earnings. A retained earnings statement is required by Generally Accepted Accounting Principles whenever comparative balance sheets and income statements are presented.

a. Financial statements
b. Notes to the financial statements
c. 3M Company
d. Statement of retained earnings

33. The term '_________' refers to the concept of collecting information and attempting to spot a pattern in the information. In some fields of study, the term '_________' has more formally-defined meanings.

In project management _________ is a mathematical technique that uses historical results to predict future outcome.

a. Regression analysis
b. Trend analysis
c. Multicollinearity
d. 3M Company

34. _________ is the balance of the amounts of cash being received and paid by a business during a defined period of time, sometimes tied to a specific project. Measurement of _________ can be used

- to evaluate the state or performance of a business or project.
- to determine problems with liquidity. Being profitable does not necessarily mean being liquid. A company can fail because of a shortage of cash, even while profitable.
- to project rate of returns. The time of _________s into and out of projects are used as inputs to financial models such as internal rate of return, and net present value.
- to examine income or growth of a business when it is believed that accrual accounting concepts do not represent economic realities. Alternately, _________ can be used to 'validate' the net income generated by accrual accounting.

_________ as a generic term may be used differently depending on context, and certain _________ definitions may be adapted by analysts and users for their own uses. Common terms include operating _________ and free _________.

a. Controlling interest
b. Commercial paper
c. Cash Flow
d. Flow-through entity

35. In financial accounting, a _________ or Statement of cash flows is a financial statement that shows a company's flow of cash. The money coming into the business is called cash inflow, and money going out from the business is called cash outflow. The statement shows how changes in balance sheet and income accounts affect cash and cash equivalents, and breaks the analysis down to operating, investing, and financing activities.

a. 3M Company
b. Cash flow statement
c. BNSF Railway
d. BMC Software, Inc.

36. In accounting, _________ or sales profit is the difference between revenue and the cost of making a product or providing a service, before deducting overhead, payroll, taxation, and interest payments. Note that this is different from operating profit (earnings before interest and taxes.)

Net sales are calculated:

Net sales = Sales - Sales returns and allowances.

a. Participating preferred stock
b. Capital structure
c. Gross profit
d. Commercial paper

37. _________ is a financial ratio used to assess the profitability of a firm's core activities, excluding fixed costs.

The general calculation is:

>

The _________ is related to the net profit margin, which assesses the profitability of an organization after including fixed costs.

_________ indicates the relationship between net sales revenue and the cost of goods sold.

a. Commercial paper
b. Gross income
c. Participating preferred stock
d. Gross profit margin

38. In business and finance accounting, _________ is equal to the gross profit minus overheads minus interest payable plus/minus one off items for a given time period (usually: accounting period.)

A common synonym for '_________' when discussing financial statements (which include a balance sheet and an income statement) is the bottom line. This term results from the traditional appearance of an income statement which shows all allocated revenues and expenses over a specified time period with the resulting summation on the bottom line of the report.

a. Salvage value
b. Cost of goods sold
c. Net profit
d. Treasury stock

39. _________, net margin, net _________ or net profit ratio all refer to a measure of profitability. It is calculated by finding the net profit as a percentage of the revenue.

$$\text{Net profit margin} = \frac{\text{Net profit (after taxes)}}{\text{Revenue}} \times 100$$

The _________ is mostly used for internal comparison.

a. BNSF Railway
b. BMC Software, Inc.
c. 3M Company
d. Profit margin

40. In business and accounting, _________ are everything of value that is owned by a person or company. It is a claim on the property your income of a borrower. The balance sheet of a firm records the monetary value of the _________ owned by the firm.

a. Earnings before interest, taxes, depreciation and amortization
b. Accounts receivable
c. Accrual basis accounting
d. Assets

41. In finance, _________ also known as return on investment, rate of profit or sometimes just return, is the ratio of money gained or lost on an investment relative to the amount of money invested. The amount of money gained or lost may be referred to as interest, profit/loss, gain/loss, or net income/loss. The money invested may be referred to as the asset, capital, principal, or the cost basis of the investment.

a. Rate of return
b. Debt to capital ratio
c. Theoretical ex-rights price
d. Capital employed

42. _________ is that which is owed; usually referencing assets owed, but the term can also cover moral obligations and other interactions not requiring money. In the case of assets, _________ is a means of using future purchasing power in the present before a summation has been earned. Some companies and corporations use _________ as a part of their overall corporate finance strategy.
a. Debenture
b. Debt
c. Lender
d. Loan

43. The _________ is a financial ratio indicating the relative proportion of equity to all used to finance a company's assets. The two components are often taken from the firm's balance sheet or statement of financial position (so-called book value), but the ratio may also be calculated using market values for both, if the company's equities are publicly traded.

The _________ is especially in Central Europe a very common financial ratio while in the US the debt to _________ is more often used in financial (research) reports.

a. Average accounting return
b. Earnings yield
c. Efficiency ratio
d. Equity ratio

44. The _________ percentage shows how profitable a company's assets are in generating revenue.

_________ can be computed as:

$$\text{ROA} = \frac{\text{Net Income - Interest Expense - Interest Tax savings}}{\text{Average Total Assets}}$$

This number tells you what the company can do with what it has, i.e. how many dollars of earnings they derive from each dollar of assets they control. Its a useful number for comparing competing companies in the same industry.

a. Capital employed
b. Statutory Liquidity Ratio
c. Return on sales
d. Return on assets

45. _________ are the earnings returned on the initial investment amount.

In the US, the Financial Accounting Standards Board (FASB) requires companies' income statements to report _________ for each of the major categories of the income statement: continuing operations, discontinued operations, extraordinary items, and net income.

The _________ formula does not include preferred dividends for categories outside of continued operations and net income.

a. Earnings per share
b. Average accounting return
c. Invested capital
d. Earnings yield

46. _________ is the fraction of net income a firm pays to its stockholders in dividends:

The part of the earnings not paid to investors is left for investment to provide for future earnings growth. Investors seeking high current income and limited capital growth prefer companies with high _________. However investors seeking capital growth may prefer lower payout ratio because capital gains are taxed at a lower rate.

a. Dividends
b. Dividend yield
c. Dividend payout ratio
d. Dividend stripping

47. A _________ is an annual report required by the U.S. Securities and Exchange Commission (SEC), that gives a comprehensive summary of a public company's performance. Although similarly named, the annual report on _________ is distinct from the often glossy 'annual report to shareholders', which a company must send to its shareholders when it holds an annual meeting to elect directors (though some companies combine the annual report and the 10-K into one document.) The 10-K includes information such as company history, organizational structure, executive compensation, equity, subsidiaries, and audited financial statements, among other information.

a. 3M Company
b. Form 10-Q
c. Form 8-K
d. Form 10-K

1. _________ of something is, in finance, the adding together of interest or different investments over a period of time such as atoms (1 - the act or process of accruing; 2 - the amount that accrues.) It holds specific meanings in accounting and payroll.

_________, in accounting, describes the accounting method known as _________ basis, whereby revenues and expenses are recognized when they are accrued, i.e. accumulated (earned or incurred), regardless when the actual cash is received or paid out.

a. Accounts receivable
b. Assets
c. Earnings before interest, taxes, depreciation and amortization
d. Accrual

2. _________ is a method of accounting whereby economic activities (rather than cash flow) of financial events are considered, because of two complementary principles, which (together) determine the point, at which expenses and revenues are recognized. According to revenue recognition principle, revenues are realized when earned, whether or not they are received in cash.

a. Earnings before interest, taxes, depreciation and amortization
b. Accrual
c. Accrued revenue
d. Accrual basis accounting

3. _________ is a company's financial statement that indicates how the revenue is transformed into the net income The purpose of the _________ is to show managers and investors whether the company made or lost money during the period being reported.

The important thing to remember about an _________ is that it represents a period of time.

a. AIG
b. ABC Television Network
c. AMEX
d. Income Statement

4. _________ is a method of accounting whereby cash flow of financial events is considered. The method recognizes revenues when cash is received and recognizes expenses when cash is paid out. In cash accounting, revenues and expenses are also called cash receipts and cash payments respectively.

a. Closing entries
b. Treasury stock
c. Cash basis accounting
d. Net sales

5. In accounting, _________ has a very specific meaning. It is an outflow of cash or other valuable assets from a person or company to another person or company. This outflow of cash is generally one side of a trade for products or services that have equal or better current or future value to the buyer than to the seller.
a. ABC Television Network
b. AMEX
c. AIG
d. Expense

6. In financial accounting, a _________ or statement of financial position is a summary of a person's or organization's balances. Assets, liabilities and ownership equity are listed as of a specific date, such as the end of its financial year. A _________ is often described as a snapshot of a company's financial condition.
a. Statement of retained earnings
b. 3M Company
c. Financial statements
d. Balance Sheet

7. _________ principle is a cornerstone of accrual accounting together with matching principle. They both determine the accounting period, in which revenues and expenses are recognized. According to the principle, revenues are recognized when they are (1) realized or realizable, and are (2) earned (usually when goods are transferred or services rendered), no matter when cash is received.
a. Net realizable value
b. 3M Company
c. BMC Software, Inc.
d. Revenue recognition

8. An _________ is a comprehensive report on a company's activities throughout the preceding year. _________s are intended to give shareholders and other interested persons information about the company's activities and financial performance. Most jurisdictions require companies to prepare and disclose _________s, and many require the _________ to be filed at the company's registry.

a. AMEX
b. ABC Television Network
c. Annual Report
d. AIG

9. A _________ is the pinnacle activity involved in selling products or services in return for money or other compensation. It is an act of completion of a commercial activity.

A _________ is completed by the seller, the owner of the goods.

a. Maturity
b. High yield stock
c. Sale
d. Tertiary sector of economy

10. _________ are formal records of a business' financial activities.

In British English, including United Kingdom company law, _________ are often referred to as accounts, although the term _________ is also used, particularly by accountants.

_________ provide an overview of a business' financial condition in both short and long term.

a. Notes to the financial statements
b. Financial statements
c. Statement of retained earnings
d. 3M Company

11. A _________ is used in research to outline possible courses of action or to present a preferred approach to an idea or thought. For example, the philosopher Isaiah Berlin used the 'hedgehogs' versus 'foxes' approach; a 'hedgehog' might approach the world in terms of a single organizing principle; a 'fox' might pursue multiple conflicting goals simultaneously. Alternatively, an empiricist might approach a subject by direct examination, whereas an intuitionist might simply intuit what's next.
a. BMC Software, Inc.
b. 3M Company
c. BNSF Railway
d. Conceptual Framework

12. _________ is a term used in accounting, economics and finance to spread the cost of an asset over the span of several years.

In simple words we can say that _________ is the reduction in the value of an asset due to usage, passage of time, wear and tear, technological outdating or obsolescence, depletion, inadequacy, rot, rust, decay or other such factors.

In accounting, _________ is a term used to describe any method of attributing the historical or purchase cost of an asset across its useful life, roughly corresponding to normal wear and tear.

a. General ledger
b. Current asset
c. Net profit
d. Depreciation

13. _________ are payments made by a corporation to its shareholder members. It is the portion of corporate profits paid out to stockholders. When a corporation earns a profit or surplus, that money can be put to two uses: it can either be re-invested in the business (called retained earnings), or it can be paid to the shareholders as a dividend.

a. Dividend payout ratio
b. Dividend yield
c. Dividends
d. Dividend stripping

14. The _________ is one of the basic financial statements as per Generally Accepted Accounting Principles, and it explains the changes in a company's retained earnings over the reporting period. It breaks down changes affecting the account, such as profits or losses from operations, dividends paid, and any other items charged or credited to retained earnings. A retained earnings statement is required by Generally Accepted Accounting Principles whenever comparative balance sheets and income statements are presented.

a. 3M Company
b. Notes to the financial statements
c. Financial statements
d. Statement of retained earnings

15. There are several methods for calculating depreciation, generally based on either the passage of time or the level of activity (or use) of the asset.

_________ is the simplest and most often used technique, in which the company estimates the salvage value of the asset at the end of the period during which it will be used to generate revenues (useful life), and will expense a portion of original cost in equal increments over that period.

a. Pro forma
b. Closing entries
c. Straight-line depreciation
d. Current asset

16. In economics, business, retail, and accounting, a _________ is the value of money that has been used up to produce something, and hence is not available for use anymore. In economics, a _________ is an alternative that is given up as a result of a decision. In business, the _________ may be one of acquisition, in which case the amount of money expended to acquire it is counted as _________.
a. Cost of quality
b. Cost allocation
c. Prime cost
d. Cost

17. In financial accounting, _________ or cost of sales includes the direct costs attributable to the production of the goods sold by a company. This amount includes the materials cost used in creating the goods along with the direct labor costs used to produce the good. It excludes indirect expenses such as distribution costs and sales force costs.
a. FIFO and LIFO accounting
b. Reorder point
c. 3M Company
d. Cost of goods sold

18. _________ is a fee paid on borrowed assets. It is the price paid for the use of borrowed money , or, money earned by deposited funds .Assets that are sometimes lent with _________ include money, shares, consumer goods through hire purchase, major assets such as aircraft, and even entire factories in finance lease arrangements. The _________ is calculated upon the value of the assets in the same manner as upon money.
a. ABC Television Network
b. AIG
c. Insolvency
d. Interest

19. A _________ is a compensation, usually financial, received by a worker in exchange for their labor.

Compensation in terms of _________s is given to worker and compensation in terms of salary is given to employees. Compensation is a monetary benefits given to employees in returns of the services provided by them.

a. Wage
b. 3M Company
c. Retirement plan
d. BMC Software, Inc.

20. The term '_________' refers to the concept of collecting information and attempting to spot a pattern in the information. In some fields of study, the term '_________' has more formally-defined meanings.

In project management _________ is a mathematical technique that uses historical results to predict future outcome.

a. 3M Company
b. Regression analysis
c. Multicollinearity
d. Trend analysis

21. _________ is a file or account that contains money that a person or company owes to suppliers, but has not paid yet (a form of debt.) When you receive an invoice you add it to the file, and then you remove it when you pay. Thus, the A/P is a form of credit that suppliers offer to their purchasers by allowing them to pay for a product or service after it has already been received.
a. Accrual
b. Accounts receivable
c. Earnings before interest, taxes, depreciation and amortization
d. Accounts payable

22. _________ is one of a series of accounting transactions dealing with the billing of customers who owe money to a person, company or organization for goods and services that have been provided to the customer. In most business entities this is typically done by generating an invoice and mailing or electronically delivering it to the customer, who in turn must pay it within an established timeframe called credit or payment terms.

An example of a common payment term is Net 30, meaning payment is due in the amount of the invoice 30 days from the date of invoice.

a. Accrued revenue
b. Adjusting entries
c. Accounts receivable
d. Accrual

23. Book Value = Original Cost - _________

Book value at the end of year becomes book value at the beginning of next year. The asset is depreciated until the book value equals scrap value.

If the vehicle were to be sold and the sales price exceeded the depreciated value (net book value) then the excess would be considered a gain and subject to depreciation recapture.

a. AMEX
b. ABC Television Network
c. AIG
d. Accumulated depreciation

24. _________ is the term used to refer to the standard framework of guidelines for financial accounting used in any given jurisdiction. _________ includes the standards, conventions, and rules accountants follow in recording and summarizing transactions, and in the preparation of financial statements.

Financial accounting information must be assembled and reported objectively.

a. Generally accepted accounting principles
b. General ledger
c. Current asset
d. Long-term liabilities

1. The term _________, derived from the distinctive T shape, is frequently used when discussing or analyzing accounting or business transactions. _________s are used to represent general ledger accounts.

Typically one or more Ts are drawn on a white board or blank piece of paper. A general ledger account name or number is then written above each T. Debit entries are recorded on the left side of the 'T' and credit entries are recorded on the right side of the 'T'.

a. BNSF Railway
b. BMC Software, Inc.
c. 3M Company
d. T account

2. _________ is a list of the accounts including a unique number of each allowing to locate it in each ledger. The list is typically arranged in the order of the customary appearance of accounts in the financial statements. A _________ can track a specific financial information.

a. Chart of accounts
b. General ledger
c. Journal entry
d. General journal

3. The _________, sometimes known as the nominal ledger, is the main accounting record of a business which uses double-entry bookkeeping. It will usually include accounts for such items as current assets, fixed assets, liabilities, revenue and expense items, gains and losses.

The _________ is a collection of the group of accounts that supports the items shown in the major financial statements.

a. General journal
b. General ledger
c. Journal entry
d. Sales journal

4. _________ is the recording of the value of assets, liabilities, income, and expenses in the daybooks, journals, and ledgers, in which debit and credit entries are chronologically posted to record changes in value. _________ is often mistaken for accounting, which is the system of recording, verifying, and reporting such information. Practitioners of accounting are called accountants.

a. Double-entry bookkeeping
b. Controlling account
c. Bookkeeping
d. Debit and credit

5. _________ is the balance of the amounts of cash being received and paid by a business during a defined period of time, sometimes tied to a specific project. Measurement of _________ can be used

- to evaluate the state or performance of a business or project.
- to determine problems with liquidity. Being profitable does not necessarily mean being liquid. A company can fail because of a shortage of cash, even while profitable.
- to project rate of returns. The time of _________s into and out of projects are used as inputs to financial models such as internal rate of return, and net present value.
- to examine income or growth of a business when it is believed that accrual accounting concepts do not represent economic realities. Alternately, _________ can be used to 'validate' the net income generated by accrual accounting.

_________ as a generic term may be used differently depending on context, and certain _________ definitions may be adapted by analysts and users for their own uses. Common terms include operating _________ and free _________.

a. Commercial paper
b. Controlling interest
c. Flow-through entity
d. Cash Flow

6. _________ is a system of financial accounting where each transaction is recorded in at least two accounts: at least one account is debited and at least one account is credited, so that the total debits of the transaction equal to the total credits. For example, if Company A sells an item to Company B, and Company B pays by cheque, then the bookkeeper of Company A credits the account 'Sales' and debits the account 'Bank'. Conversely, the bookkeeper of Company B debits the account 'Purchases' and credits the account 'Bank'.
a. Double-entry bookkeeping
b. Cookie jar accounting
c. Bookkeeping
d. Debit and credit

7. _________ is a company's financial statement that indicates how the revenue is transformed into the net income The purpose of the _________ is to show managers and investors whether the company made or lost money during the period being reported.

The important thing to remember about an _________ is that it represents a period of time.

a. ABC Television Network
b. Income Statement
c. AMEX
d. AIG

8. In financial accounting, a _________ or Statement of cash flows is a financial statement that shows a company's flow of cash. The money coming into the business is called cash inflow, and money going out from the business is called cash outflow. The statement shows how changes in balance sheet and income accounts affect cash and cash equivalents, and breaks the analysis down to operating, investing, and financing activities.
a. 3M Company
b. BNSF Railway
c. BMC Software, Inc.
d. Cash flow statement

9. An _________ invented by esteemed professor Karen Osterheld is the system of records a business keeps to maintain its accounting system. This includes the purchase, sales, and other financial processes of the business. The purpose of an _________ is to accumulate data and provide decision makers (investors, creditors, and managers) with information to make decision While this was previously a paper-based process, most modern businesses now use accounting software such as UBS, MYOB etc.
a. Accounting information system
b. ABC Television Network
c. AIG
d. AMEX

10. The _________ is where double entry bookkeeping entries are recorded by debiting one account and crediting another account with the same amount. The amount debited and the amount credited should always be equal, thereby ensuring the accounting equation is maintained.

Depending on the business's accounting information system, specialized journals may be used in conjunction with the _________ for record-keeping.

a. Journal entry
b. General ledger
c. Sales journal
d. General journal

11. A _________ has several related meanings:

- a daily record of events or business; a private _________ is usually referred to as a diary.
- a newspaper or other periodical, in the literal sense of one published each day;
- many publications issued at stated intervals, such as magazines, or scholarly academic _________s, or the record of the transactions of a society, are often called _________s. Although _________ is sometimes used, erroneously, as a synonym for 'magazine,' in academic use, a _________ refers to a serious, scholarly publication, most often peer-reviewed. A non-scholarly magazine written for an educated audience about an industry or an area of professional activity is usually called a professional magazine.

The word 'journalist' for one whose business is writing for the public press has been in use since the end of the 17th century.

Open access _________s are scholarly _________s that are available to the reader without financial or other barrier other than access to the internet itself. Some are subsidized, and some require payment on behalf of the author. Subsidized _________s are financed by an academic institution or a government information center.

a. BNSF Railway
b. Journal
c. BMC Software, Inc.
d. 3M Company

12. In accounting, the _________ is a worksheet listing the balance at a certain date, of each ledger account in two columns, namely debit and credit. Under the double-entry system, in any transaction the total of any debits must equal the total of any credits, so in a _________ the total of the debit side should always be equal to the total of the credit side. The _________ thus serves as a tool to detect errors, which can result in the totals not being equal.

a. Trial balance
b. Current asset
c. Depreciation
d. Bottom line

13. A _________ is used in research to outline possible courses of action or to present a preferred approach to an idea or thought. For example, the philosopher Isaiah Berlin used the 'hedgehogs' versus 'foxes' approach; a 'hedgehog' might approach the world in terms of a single organizing principle; a 'fox' might pursue multiple conflicting goals simultaneously. Alternatively, an empiricist might approach a subject by direct examination, whereas an intuitionist might simply intuit what's next.

a. BNSF Railway
b. Conceptual Framework
c. 3M Company
d. BMC Software, Inc.

14. _________ are formal records of a business' financial activities.

In British English, including United Kingdom company law, _________ are often referred to as accounts, although the term _________ is also used, particularly by accountants.

_________ provide an overview of a business' financial condition in both short and long term.

a. Statement of retained earnings
b. 3M Company
c. Notes to the financial statements
d. Financial statements

15. _________ are journal entries made at the end of an accounting period to transfer temporary accounts to permanent accounts. An 'income summary' account may be used to show the balance between revenue and expenses, or they could be directly closed against retained earnings where dividend payments will be deducted from. This process is used to reset the balance of these temporary accounts to zero for the next accounting period.

a. FIFO and LIFO accounting
b. Trial balance
c. Treasury stock
d. Closing entries

16. In financial accounting, a _________ or statement of financial position is a summary of a person's or organization's balances. Assets, liabilities and ownership equity are listed as of a specific date, such as the end of its financial year. A _________ is often described as a snapshot of a company's financial condition.

a. Statement of retained earnings
b. 3M Company
c. Financial statements
d. Balance Sheet

17. In business and accounting, _________ are everything of value that is owned by a person or company. It is a claim on the property your income of a borrower. The balance sheet of a firm records the monetary value of the _________ owned by the firm.

a. Accounts receivable
b. Earnings before interest, taxes, depreciation and amortization
c. Accrual basis accounting
d. Assets

18. The basic _________ is the foundation for the double-entry bookkeeping system. It shows how assets were financed: either by borrowing money from someone (liability) or by paying your own money (shareholders' equity.)

Assets = Liabilities + (Shareholders or Owners equity)

For example: A student buys a computer for $945.

a. ABC Television Network
b. AIG
c. AMEX
d. Accounting equation

19. _________ and credit are formal bookkeeping and accounting terms. They are the most fundamental concepts in accounting, representing the two records that one party in a transaction makes on its records, transferring a money balance from one account to another, one representing a reduction of liability or increase in asset, and the other representing a balancing increase in liability or reduction of asset.

Introduction

_________s and credits are a system of notation used in accounting to keep track of money movements (transactions) into and out of an account.

a. Cookie jar accounting
b. Debit
c. Bookkeeping
d. Debit and credit

20. _________ are payments made by a corporation to its shareholder members. It is the portion of corporate profits paid out to stockholders. When a corporation earns a profit or surplus, that money can be put to two uses: it can either be re-invested in the business (called retained earnings), or it can be paid to the shareholders as a dividend.

a. Dividend stripping
b. Dividend payout ratio
c. Dividend yield
d. Dividends

21. In accounting, _________ has a very specific meaning. It is an outflow of cash or other valuable assets from a person or company to another person or company. This outflow of cash is generally one side of a trade for products or services that have equal or better current or future value to the buyer than to the seller.

a. AIG
b. ABC Television Network
c. AMEX
d. Expense

22. In economics, the _________, (or _________) measures the payments that flow between any individual country and all other countries. It is used to summarize all international economic transactions for that country during a specific time period, usually a year. The _________ is determined by the country's exports and imports of goods, services, and financial capital, as well as financial transfers.

a. Yield to maturity
b. Stock split
c. Moving average
d. Balance of payments

23. _________ of something is, in finance, the adding together of interest or different investments over a period of time such as atoms (1 - the act or process of accruing; 2 - the amount that accrues.) It holds specific meanings in accounting and payroll.

_________, in accounting, describes the accounting method known as _________ basis, whereby revenues and expenses are recognized when they are accrued, i.e. accumulated (earned or incurred), regardless when the actual cash is received or paid out.

a. Accrual
b. Assets
c. Earnings before interest, taxes, depreciation and amortization
d. Accounts receivable

24. _________ is a method of accounting whereby economic activities (rather than cash flow) of financial events are considered, because of two complementary principles, which (together) determine the point, at which expenses and revenues are recognized. According to revenue recognition principle, revenues are realized when earned, whether or not they are received in cash.

a. Accrual basis accounting
b. Accrued revenue
c. Accrual
d. Earnings before interest, taxes, depreciation and amortization

25. _________ is a method of accounting whereby cash flow of financial events is considered. The method recognizes revenues when cash is received and recognizes expenses when cash is paid out. In cash accounting, revenues and expenses are also called cash receipts and cash payments respectively.

a. Treasury stock
b. Closing entries
c. Net sales
d. Cash basis accounting

26. In economics, _________ or _________ goods or real _________ refers to factors of production used to create goods or services that are not themselves significantly consumed (though they may depreciate) in the production process. _________ goods may be acquired with money or financial _________. In finance and accounting, _________ generally refers to financial wealth, especially that used to start or maintain a business.

a. Disclosure
b. Screening
c. Vyborg Appeal
d. Capital

27. In finance, _________ refers to the way a corporation finances its assets through some combination of equity, debt, or hybrid securities. A firm's _________ is then the composition or 'structure' of its liabilities. For example, a firm that sells $20 billion in equity and $80 billion in debt is said to be 20% equity-financed and 80% debt-financed.

a. Capital structure
b. Restricted stock
c. Gross income
d. Flow-through entity

28. _________ is that which is owed; usually referencing assets owed, but the term can also cover moral obligations and other interactions not requiring money. In the case of assets, _________ is a means of using future purchasing power in the present before a summation has been earned. Some companies and corporations use _________ as a part of their overall corporate finance strategy.

a. Debt
b. Debenture
c. Lender
d. Loan

29. _________, in law and economics, is a form of risk management primarily used to hedge against the risk of a contingent loss. _________ is defined as the equitable transfer of the risk of a loss, from one entity to another, in exchange for a premium, and can be thought of as a guaranteed small loss to prevent a large, possibly devastating loss. An insurer is a company selling the _________; an insured is the person or entity buying the _________.

a. AIG
b. AMEX
c. ABC Television Network
d. Insurance

30. A _________, also referred to as a note payable in accounting, is a contract where one party (the maker or issuer) makes an unconditional promise in writing to pay a sum of money to the other (the payee), either at a fixed or determinable future time or on demand of the payee, under specific terms. They differ from IOUs in that they contain a specific promise to pay, rather than simply acknowledging that a debt exists.

The terms of a note typically include the principal amount, the interest rate if any, and the maturity date.

a. BNSF Railway
b. Promissory note
c. BMC Software, Inc.
d. 3M Company

31. A _________ is the pinnacle activity involved in selling products or services in return for money or other compensation. It is an act of completion of a commercial activity.

A _________ is completed by the seller, the owner of the goods.

a. High yield stock
b. Tertiary sector of economy
c. Sale
d. Maturity

32. An account statement or a _________ is a summary of all financial transactions occurring over a given period of time on a deposit account, a credit card, or any other type of account offered by a financial institution.

_________s are typically printed on one or several pieces of paper and either mailed directly to the account holder's address, or kept at the financial institution's local branch for pick-up. Certain ATMs offer the possibility to print, at any time, a condensed version of a _________.

a. BNSF Railway
b. 3M Company
c. Bank statement
d. BMC Software, Inc.

33. _________ is one of a series of accounting transactions dealing with the billing of customers who owe money to a person, company or organization for goods and services that have been provided to the customer. In most business entities this is typically done by generating an invoice and mailing or electronically delivering it to the customer, who in turn must pay it within an established timeframe called credit or payment terms.

An example of a common payment term is Net 30, meaning payment is due in the amount of the invoice 30 days from the date of invoice.

a. Adjusting entries
b. Accrual
c. Accounts receivable
d. Accrued revenue

34. _________ is a file or account that contains money that a person or company owes to suppliers, but has not paid yet (a form of debt.) When you receive an invoice you add it to the file, and then you remove it when you pay. Thus, the A/P is a form of credit that suppliers offer to their purchasers by allowing them to pay for a product or service after it has already been received.

a. Earnings before interest, taxes, depreciation and amortization
b. Accounts payable
c. Accrual
d. Accounts receivable

35. _________ is a term used in accounting, economics and finance to spread the cost of an asset over the span of several years.

In simple words we can say that _________ is the reduction in the value of an asset due to usage, passage of time, wear and tear, technological outdating or obsolescence, depletion, inadequacy, rot, rust, decay or other such factors.

In accounting, _________ is a term used to describe any method of attributing the historical or purchase cost of an asset across its useful life, roughly corresponding to normal wear and tear.

a. General ledger
b. Depreciation
c. Current asset
d. Net profit

36. _________ is a fee paid on borrowed assets. It is the price paid for the use of borrowed money , or, money earned by deposited funds .Assets that are sometimes lent with _________ include money, shares, consumer goods through hire purchase, major assets such as aircraft, and even entire factories in finance lease arrangements. The _________ is calculated upon the value of the assets in the same manner as upon money.

a. Insolvency
b. AIG
c. ABC Television Network
d. Interest

37. _________, in accrual accounting, (e.g. advance payment received from a client) is, according to revenue recognition, revenue not earned until the delivery of goods or services, which until then, is still owed to the payer, hence remaining a liability.

_________, sometimes referred to as deferred revenue or unearned revenue, shares characteristics with accrued expense with the difference that a liability to be covered latter is cash received FROM a counterpart, while goods or services are to be delivered in a latter period, when such income item is earned, the related revenue item is recognized, and the same amount is deducted from deferred revenues.

a. Treasury stock
b. Matching principle
c. Gross sales
d. Deferred income

38. The term '_________' refers to the concept of collecting information and attempting to spot a pattern in the information. In some fields of study, the term '_________' has more formally-defined meanings.

In project management _________ is a mathematical technique that uses historical results to predict future outcome.

a. 3M Company
b. Multicollinearity
c. Regression analysis
d. Trend analysis

39. A _________ is an annual report required by the U.S. Securities and Exchange Commission (SEC), that gives a comprehensive summary of a public company's performance. Although similarly named, the annual report on _________ is distinct from the often glossy 'annual report to shareholders', which a company must send to its shareholders when it holds an annual meeting to elect directors (though some companies combine the annual report and the 10-K into one document.) The 10-K includes information such as company history, organizational structure, executive compensation, equity, subsidiaries, and audited financial statements, among other information.

a. 3M Company
b. Form 10-Q
c. Form 8-K
d. Form 10-K

1. An _________ is a comprehensive report on a company's activities throughout the preceding year. _________s are intended to give shareholders and other interested persons information about the company's activities and financial performance. Most jurisdictions require companies to prepare and disclose _________s, and many require the _________ to be filed at the company's registry.

a. Annual Report
b. AMEX
c. ABC Television Network
d. AIG

2. In financial accounting, a _________ or statement of financial position is a summary of a person's or organization's balances. Assets, liabilities and ownership equity are listed as of a specific date, such as the end of its financial year. A _________ is often described as a snapshot of a company's financial condition.

a. 3M Company
b. Financial statements
c. Balance Sheet
d. Statement of retained earnings

3. _________ is a company's financial statement that indicates how the revenue is transformed into the net income The purpose of the _________ is to show managers and investors whether the company made or lost money during the period being reported.

The important thing to remember about an _________ is that it represents a period of time.

a. Income Statement
b. AIG
c. AMEX
d. ABC Television Network

4. _________ is a term used in accounting, economics and finance to spread the cost of an asset over the span of several years.

In simple words we can say that _________ is the reduction in the value of an asset due to usage, passage of time, wear and tear, technological outdating or obsolescence, depletion, inadequacy, rot, rust, decay or other such factors.

In accounting, _________ is a term used to describe any method of attributing the historical or purchase cost of an asset across its useful life, roughly corresponding to normal wear and tear.

a. General ledger
b. Net profit
c. Current asset
d. Depreciation

5. In physics, and more specifically kinematics, _________ is the change in velocity over time. Because velocity is a vector, it can change in two ways: a change in magnitude and/or a change in direction. In one dimension, _________ is the rate at which something speeds up or slows down.
a. Acceleration
b. ABC Television Network
c. AIG
d. AMEX

6. The _________ is the current method of accelerated asset depreciation required by the United States income tax code. Under _________, all assets are divided into classes which dictate the number of years over which an asset's cost will be recovered.

Prior to the Accelerated Cost Recovery System (ACRS), most capital purchases were depreciated using a straight line technique, that allowed for the depreciation of the asset over its useful life.

a. Categorical grants
b. Modified Accelerated Cost Recovery System
c. BMC Software, Inc.
d. 3M Company

7. In economics, business, retail, and accounting, a _________ is the value of money that has been used up to produce something, and hence is not available for use anymore. In economics, a _________ is an alternative that is given up as a result of a decision. In business, the _________ may be one of acquisition, in which case the amount of money expended to acquire it is counted as _________.
a. Cost
b. Prime cost
c. Cost of quality
d. Cost allocation

8. _________ is the term used to refer to the standard framework of guidelines for financial accounting used in any given jurisdiction. _________ includes the standards, conventions, and rules accountants follow in recording and summarizing transactions, and in the preparation of financial statements.

Financial accounting information must be assembled and reported objectively.

a. Current asset
b. Long-term liabilities
c. General ledger
d. Generally accepted accounting principles

9. The term _________, derived from the distinctive T shape, is frequently used when discussing or analyzing accounting or business transactions. _________s are used to represent general ledger accounts.

Typically one or more Ts are drawn on a white board or blank piece of paper. A general ledger account name or number is then written above each T. Debit entries are recorded on the left side of the 'T' and credit entries are recorded on the right side of the 'T'.

a. BNSF Railway
b. T account
c. 3M Company
d. BMC Software, Inc.

10. _________ of something is, in finance, the adding together of interest or different investments over a period of time such as atoms (1 - the act or process of accruing; 2 - the amount that accrues.) It holds specific meanings in accounting and payroll.

_________, in accounting, describes the accounting method known as _________ basis, whereby revenues and expenses are recognized when they are accrued, i.e. accumulated (earned or incurred), regardless when the actual cash is received or paid out.

a. Accrual
b. Assets
c. Earnings before interest, taxes, depreciation and amortization
d. Accounts receivable

11. _________ is a method of accounting whereby economic activities (rather than cash flow) of financial events are considered, because of two complementary principles, which (together) determine the point, at which expenses and revenues are recognized. According to revenue recognition principle, revenues are realized when earned, whether or not they are received in cash.

a. Accrued revenue
b. Earnings before interest, taxes, depreciation and amortization
c. Accrual
d. Accrual basis accounting

12. Book Value = Original Cost - _________

Book value at the end of year becomes book value at the beginning of next year. The asset is depreciated until the book value equals scrap value.

If the vehicle were to be sold and the sales price exceeded the depreciated value (net book value) then the excess would be considered a gain and subject to depreciation recapture.

a. AMEX
b. ABC Television Network
c. AIG
d. Accumulated depreciation

13. _________ are payments made by a corporation to its shareholder members. It is the portion of corporate profits paid out to stockholders. When a corporation earns a profit or surplus, that money can be put to two uses: it can either be re-invested in the business (called retained earnings), or it can be paid to the shareholders as a dividend.
a. Dividend payout ratio
b. Dividend stripping
c. Dividend yield
d. Dividends

14. The _________ is one of the basic financial statements as per Generally Accepted Accounting Principles, and it explains the changes in a company's retained earnings over the reporting period. It breaks down changes affecting the account, such as profits or losses from operations, dividends paid, and any other items charged or credited to retained earnings. A retained earnings statement is required by Generally Accepted Accounting Principles whenever comparative balance sheets and income statements are presented.
a. Notes to the financial statements
b. Statement of retained earnings
c. 3M Company
d. Financial statements

15. There are several methods for calculating depreciation, generally based on either the passage of time or the level of activity (or use) of the asset.

_________ is the simplest and most often used technique, in which the company estimates the salvage value of the asset at the end of the period during which it will be used to generate revenues (useful life), and will expense a portion of original cost in equal increments over that period.

a. Pro forma
b. Straight-line depreciation
c. Closing entries
d. Current asset

16. In accounting, _________ is the original monetary value of an economic item. In some circumstances, assets and liabilities may be shown at their _________, as if there had been no change in value since the date of acquisition. The balance sheet value of the item may therefore differ from the 'true' value.
a. Historical cost
b. Bottom line
c. Cost of goods sold
d. Matching principle

17. _________ was a maxim coined by Josiah Warren, indicating a (prescriptive) version of the labor theory of value. Warren maintained that the just compensation for labor (or for its product) could only be an equivalent amount of labor (or a product embodying an equivalent amount.) Thus, profit, rent, and interest were considered unjust economic arrangements.
a. 3M Company
b. Politicized issue
c. BMC Software, Inc.
d. Cost the limit of price

18. In business and accounting, _________ are everything of value that is owned by a person or company. It is a claim on the property your income of a borrower. The balance sheet of a firm records the monetary value of the _________ owned by the firm.
a. Accounts receivable
b. Accrual basis accounting
c. Earnings before interest, taxes, depreciation and amortization
d. Assets

19. An _________ is a term used in behavioral economics to describe those types of behaviors that impose costs on a person in the long-run that are not taken into account when making decisions in the present. Classical Economics discourages government from creating legislation that targets internalities, because it is assumed that the consumer takes these personal costs into account when paying for the good that causes the _________. For example, cigarettes should be taxed because of the negative consumption externalities that they impose, such as second-hand smoke, not because the smoker harms him or herself by smoking.

a. Authorised capital
b. Operating budget
c. Inventory turnover ratio
d. Internality

20. The _________ is the United States federal government agency that collects taxes and enforces the internal revenue laws. It is an agency within the U.S. Dept of the treasury responsible for interpretation and application of Federal tax law. The official U.S. Treasury regulations provide (in part):

The _________ is a bureau of the Department of the Treasury under the immediate direction of the Commissioner of Internal Revenue.

a. Internal Revenue Service
b. Income tax
c. Use tax
d. Indirect tax

21. In economics, the _________, (or _________) measures the payments that flow between any individual country and all other countries. It is used to summarize all international economic transactions for that country during a specific time period, usually a year. The _________ is determined by the country's exports and imports of goods, services, and financial capital, as well as financial transfers.

a. Yield to maturity
b. Stock split
c. Moving average
d. Balance of payments

22. The _________, sometimes known as the nominal ledger, is the main accounting record of a business which uses double-entry bookkeeping. It will usually include accounts for such items as current assets, fixed assets, liabilities, revenue and expense items, gains and losses.

The _________ is a collection of the group of accounts that supports the items shown in the major financial statements.

a. Sales journal
b. General journal
c. Journal entry
d. General ledger

23. _________ is the balance of the amounts of cash being received and paid by a business during a defined period of time, sometimes tied to a specific project. Measurement of _________ can be used

- to evaluate the state or performance of a business or project.
- to determine problems with liquidity. Being profitable does not necessarily mean being liquid. A company can fail because of a shortage of cash, even while profitable.
- to project rate of returns. The time of _________s into and out of projects are used as inputs to financial models such as internal rate of return, and net present value.
- to examine income or growth of a business when it is believed that accrual accounting concepts do not represent economic realities. Alternately, _________ can be used to 'validate' the net income generated by accrual accounting.

_________ as a generic term may be used differently depending on context, and certain _________ definitions may be adapted by analysts and users for their own uses. Common terms include operating _________ and free _________.

a. Flow-through entity
b. Cash Flow
c. Controlling interest
d. Commercial paper

24. In financial accounting, a _________ or Statement of cash flows is a financial statement that shows a company's flow of cash. The money coming into the business is called cash inflow, and money going out from the business is called cash outflow. The statement shows how changes in balance sheet and income accounts affect cash and cash equivalents, and breaks the analysis down to operating, investing, and financing activities.
a. 3M Company
b. Cash flow statement
c. BNSF Railway
d. BMC Software, Inc.

25. In accounting, _________ or carrying value is the value of an asset according to its balance sheet account balance. For assets, the value is based on the original cost of the asset less any depreciation, amortization or impairment costs made against the asset. Traditionally, a company's _________ is its total assets minus intangible assets and liabilities.

a. Book value
b. Generally accepted accounting principles
c. Depreciation
d. Matching principle

26. In accounting, _________ are considered liabilities of the business that are to be settled in cash within the fiscal year or the operating cycle, whichever period is longer.

For example accounts payable for goods, services or supplies that were purchased for use in the operation of the business and payable within a normal period of time would be _________.

Bonds, mortgages and loans that are payable over a term exceeding one year would be fixed liabilities.

a. Payroll
b. Closing entries
c. Current liabilities
d. Treasury stock

27. In economic models, the _________ time frame assumes no fixed factors of production. Firms can enter or leave the marketplace, and the cost (and availability) of land, labor, raw materials, and capital goods can be assumed to vary. In contrast, in the short-run time frame, certain factors are assumed to be fixed, because there is not sufficient time for them to change.
a. 3M Company
b. Long-run
c. Short-run
d. BMC Software, Inc.

28. _________ are liabilities with a future benefit over one year, such as notes payable that mature greater than one year.

In accounting, the _________ are shown on the right wing of the balance-sheet representing the sources of funds, which are generally bounded in form of capital assets.

Examples of _________ are debentures, mortgage loans and other bank loans (note: not all bank loans are long term as not all are paid over a period greater than a year, the example is bridging loan.)

a. Cash basis accounting
b. Gross sales
c. Long-term liabilities
d. Book value

29. In financial accounting, a _________ is defined as an obligation of an entity arising from past transactions or events, the settlement of which may result in the transfer or use of assets, provision of services or other yielding of economic benefits in the future.
a. False Claims Act
b. Vested
c. Liability
d. Corporate governance

1. _________ of something is, in finance, the adding together of interest or different investments over a period of time such as atoms (1 - the act or process of accruing; 2 - the amount that accrues.) It holds specific meanings in accounting and payroll.

_________, in accounting, describes the accounting method known as _________ basis, whereby revenues and expenses are recognized when they are accrued, i.e. accumulated (earned or incurred), regardless when the actual cash is received or paid out.

a. Assets
b. Accounts receivable
c. Earnings before interest, taxes, depreciation and amortization
d. Accrual

2. _________ is a method of accounting whereby economic activities (rather than cash flow) of financial events are considered, because of two complementary principles, which (together) determine the point, at which expenses and revenues are recognized. According to revenue recognition principle, revenues are realized when earned, whether or not they are received in cash.

a. Earnings before interest, taxes, depreciation and amortization
b. Accrual
c. Accrued revenue
d. Accrual basis accounting

3. An _________ is a comprehensive report on a company's activities throughout the preceding year. _________s are intended to give shareholders and other interested persons information about the company's activities and financial performance. Most jurisdictions require companies to prepare and disclose _________s, and many require the _________ to be filed at the company's registry.

a. ABC Television Network
b. Annual Report
c. AMEX
d. AIG

4. In accounting, _________ has a very specific meaning. It is an outflow of cash or other valuable assets from a person or company to another person or company. This outflow of cash is generally one side of a trade for products or services that have equal or better current or future value to the buyer than to the seller.

a. AMEX
b. Expense
c. AIG
d. ABC Television Network

5. The _________ is a private, not-for-profit organization whose primary purpose is to develop generally accepted accounting principles (GAAP) within the United States in the public's interest. The Securities and Exchange Commission (SEC) designated the _________ as the organization responsible for setting accounting standards for public companies in the U.S. It was created in 1973, replacing the Accounting Principles Board and the Committee on Accounting Procedure of the American Institute of Certified Public Accountants. The _________'s mission is 'to establish and improve standards of financial accounting and reporting for the guidance and education of the public, including issuers, auditors, and users of financial information.'

The _________ is not a governmental body.

a. Financial Accounting Standards Board
b. Governmental Accounting Standards Board
c. Fannie Mae
d. Public company

6. _________ methods are means of managing inventory and financial matters involving the money a company ties up within inventory of produced goods, raw materials, parts, components, or feed stocks. FIFO stands for first-in, first-out, meaning that the oldest inventory items are recorded as sold first. LIFO stands for last-in, first-out, meaning that the most recently purchased items are recorded as sold first.

a. 3M Company
b. Finished good
c. FIFO and LIFO accounting
d. Reorder point

7. A _________ is the pinnacle activity involved in selling products or services in return for money or other compensation. It is an act of completion of a commercial activity.

A _________ is completed by the seller, the owner of the goods.

a. High yield stock
b. Tertiary sector of economy
c. Sale
d. Maturity

8. In economics, business, retail, and accounting, a _________ is the value of money that has been used up to produce something, and hence is not available for use anymore. In economics, a _________ is an alternative that is given up as a result of a decision. In business, the _________ may be one of acquisition, in which case the amount of money expended to acquire it is counted as _________.

a. Prime cost
b. Cost
c. Cost of quality
d. Cost allocation

9. In financial accounting, _________ or cost of sales includes the direct costs attributable to the production of the goods sold by a company. This amount includes the materials cost used in creating the goods along with the direct labor costs used to produce the good. It excludes indirect expenses such as distribution costs and sales force costs.
a. 3M Company
b. Cost of goods sold
c. FIFO and LIFO accounting
d. Reorder point

10. _________ is the balance of the amounts of cash being received and paid by a business during a defined period of time, sometimes tied to a specific project. Measurement of _________ can be used

- to evaluate the state or performance of a business or project.
- to determine problems with liquidity. Being profitable does not necessarily mean being liquid. A company can fail because of a shortage of cash, even while profitable.
- to project rate of returns. The time of _________s into and out of projects are used as inputs to financial models such as internal rate of return, and net present value.
- to examine income or growth of a business when it is believed that accrual accounting concepts do not represent economic realities. Alternately, _________ can be used to 'validate' the net income generated by accrual accounting.

_________ as a generic term may be used differently depending on context, and certain _________ definitions may be adapted by analysts and users for their own uses. Common terms include operating _________ and free _________.

a. Commercial paper
b. Flow-through entity
c. Controlling interest
d. Cash Flow

11. _________ refers to a business or organization attempting to acquire goods or services to accomplish the goals of the enterprise. Though there are several organizations that attempt to set standards in the _________ process, processes can vary greatly between organizations. Typically the word e;_________e; is not used interchangeably with the word e;procuremente;, since procurement typically includes Expediting, Supplier Quality, and Traffic and Logistics (T'L) in addition to _________.

a. Purchasing
b. Consignor
c. Supply chain
d. Free port

12. In financial accounting, a _________ or Statement of cash flows is a financial statement that shows a company's flow of cash. The money coming into the business is called cash inflow, and money going out from the business is called cash outflow. The statement shows how changes in balance sheet and income accounts affect cash and cash equivalents, and breaks the analysis down to operating, investing, and financing activities.
a. BMC Software, Inc.
b. BNSF Railway
c. 3M Company
d. Cash flow statement

13. _________ is an acronym for First In, First Out, an abstraction in ways of organizing and manipulation of data relative to time and prioritization. This expression describes the principle of a queue processing technique or servicing conflicting demands by ordering process by first-come, first-served (FCFS) behaviour: what comes in first is handled first, what comes in next waits until the first is finished, etc.

Thus it is analogous to the behaviour of persons queueing (or 'standing in line', in common American parlance), where the persons leave the queue in the order they arrive, or waiting one's turn at a traffic control signal.

a. Trademark
b. Kanban
c. FIFO
d. Risk management

14. Under the average-cost method, it is assumed that the cost of inventory is based on the _________ of the goods available for sale during the period. _________ is computed by dividing the total cost of goods available for sale by the total units available for sale. This gives a weighted-average unit cost that is applied to the units in the ending inventory.
a. Average cost
b. Ending inventory
c. AIG
d. ABC Television Network

15. Under the _________, it is assumed that the cost of inventory is based on the average cost of the goods available for sale during the period. Average cost is computed by dividing the total cost of goods available for sale by the total units available for sale. This gives a weighted-average unit cost that is applied to the units in the ending inventory.

a. AIG
b. Average-cost method
c. ABC Television Network
d. AMEX

16. _________ is a company's financial statement that indicates how the revenue is transformed into the net income The purpose of the _________ is to show managers and investors whether the company made or lost money during the period being reported.

The important thing to remember about an _________ is that it represents a period of time.

a. AMEX
b. AIG
c. ABC Television Network
d. Income Statement

17. Discounting is a financial mechanism in which a debtor obtains the right to delay payments to a creditor, for a defined period of time, in exchange for a charge or fee. Essentially, the party that owes money in the present purchases the right to delay the payment until some future date. The _________, or charge, is simply the difference between the original amount owed in the present and the amount that has to be paid in the future to settle the debt.
a. Risk aversion
b. Discounting
c. Discount
d. Discount factor

18. In economics, the _________, (or _________) measures the payments that flow between any individual country and all other countries. It is used to summarize all international economic transactions for that country during a specific time period, usually a year. The _________ is determined by the country's exports and imports of goods, services, and financial capital, as well as financial transfers.
a. Stock split
b. Yield to maturity
c. Moving average
d. Balance of payments

19. The _________, sometimes known as the nominal ledger, is the main accounting record of a business which uses double-entry bookkeeping. It will usually include accounts for such items as current assets, fixed assets, liabilities, revenue and expense items, gains and losses.

The _________ is a collection of the group of accounts that supports the items shown in the major financial statements.

a. General ledger
b. Sales journal
c. Journal entry
d. General journal

20. A _________ is an annual report required by the U.S. Securities and Exchange Commission (SEC), that gives a comprehensive summary of a public company's performance. Although similarly named, the annual report on _________ is distinct from the often glossy 'annual report to shareholders', which a company must send to its shareholders when it holds an annual meeting to elect directors (though some companies combine the annual report and the 10-K into one document.) The 10-K includes information such as company history, organizational structure, executive compensation, equity, subsidiaries, and audited financial statements, among other information.

a. Form 10-Q
b. 3M Company
c. Form 8-K
d. Form 10-K

1. An _________ is a comprehensive report on a company's activities throughout the preceding year. _________s are intended to give shareholders and other interested persons information about the company's activities and financial performance. Most jurisdictions require companies to prepare and disclose _________s, and many require the _________ to be filed at the company's registry.
   a. AIG
   b. ABC Television Network
   c. AMEX
   d. Annual Report

2. In business and accounting, _________ are everything of value that is owned by a person or company. It is a claim on the property your income of a borrower. The balance sheet of a firm records the monetary value of the _________ owned by the firm.
   a. Accrual basis accounting
   b. Assets
   c. Accounts receivable
   d. Earnings before interest, taxes, depreciation and amortization

3. In financial accounting, a _________ or statement of financial position is a summary of a person's or organization's balances. Assets, liabilities and ownership equity are listed as of a specific date, such as the end of its financial year. A _________ is often described as a snapshot of a company's financial condition.
   a. 3M Company
   b. Statement of retained earnings
   c. Financial statements
   d. Balance Sheet

4. In accounting, a _________ is an asset on the balance sheet which is expected to be sold or otherwise used up in the near future, usually within one year, or one business cycle - whichever is longer. Typical _________s include cash, cash equivalents, accounts receivable, inventory, the portion of prepaid accounts which will be used within a year, and short-term investments.

   On the balance sheet, assets will typically be classified into _________s and long-term assets.

   a. Current asset
   b. Deferred
   c. General ledger
   d. Pro forma

5. _________ and credit are formal bookkeeping and accounting terms. They are the most fundamental concepts in accounting, representing the two records that one party in a transaction makes on its records, transferring a money balance from one account to another, one representing a reduction of liability or increase in asset, and the other representing a balancing increase in liability or reduction of asset.

Introduction

_________s and credits are a system of notation used in accounting to keep track of money movements (transactions) into and out of an account.

a. Debit and credit
b. Cookie jar accounting
c. Bookkeeping
d. Debit

6. The _________ is a private, not-for-profit organization whose primary purpose is to develop generally accepted accounting principles (GAAP) within the United States in the public's interest. The Securities and Exchange Commission (SEC) designated the _________ as the organization responsible for setting accounting standards for public companies in the U.S. It was created in 1973, replacing the Accounting Principles Board and the Committee on Accounting Procedure of the American Institute of Certified Public Accountants. The _________'s mission is 'to establish and improve standards of financial accounting and reporting for the guidance and education of the public, including issuers, auditors, and users of financial information.'

The _________ is not a governmental body.

a. Governmental Accounting Standards Board
b. Fannie Mae
c. Public company
d. Financial Accounting Standards Board

7. _________ are defined as identifiable non-monetary assets that cannot be seen, touched or physically measured, which are created through time and/or effort and that are identifiable as a separate asset. There are two primary forms of intangibles - legal intangibles (such as trade secrets (e.g., customer lists), copyrights, patents, trademarks, and goodwill) and competitive intangibles (such as knowledge activities (know-how, knowledge), collaboration activities, leverage activities, and structural activities.) Legal intangibles are known under the generic term intellectual property and generate legal property rights defensible in a court of law.

a. Intangible assets
b. ABC Television Network
c. AIG
d. Overhead

8. _________ is a business, economics or investment term that refers to an asset's ability to be easily converted through an act of buying or selling without causing a significant movement in the price and with minimum loss of value. Money, or cash on hand, is the most liquid asset. An act of exchange of a less liquid asset with a more liquid asset is called liquidation.

a. Financial instruments
b. Transfer agent
c. Spot rate
d. Market liquidity

9. In economic models, the _________ time frame assumes no fixed factors of production. Firms can enter or leave the marketplace, and the cost (and availability) of land, labor, raw materials, and capital goods can be assumed to vary. In contrast, in the short-run time frame, certain factors are assumed to be fixed, because there is not sufficient time for them to change.

a. 3M Company
b. Short-run
c. BMC Software, Inc.
d. Long-run

10. _________ is any physical or virtual entity that is owned by an individual or jointly by a group of individuals. An owner of _________ has the right to consume, sell, rent, mortgage, transfer and exchange his or her _________. Important widely-recognized types of _________ include real _________, personal _________ (other physical possessions), and intellectual _________ (rights over artistic creations, inventions, etc.), although the latter is not always as widely recognized or enforced.

a. Primary authority
b. Property
c. Fiduciary
d. Disclosure requirement

11. _________ is that which is owed; usually referencing assets owed, but the term can also cover moral obligations and other interactions not requiring money. In the case of assets, _________ is a means of using future purchasing power in the present before a summation has been earned. Some companies and corporations use _________ as a part of their overall corporate finance strategy.

a. Lender
b. Debenture
c. Debt
d. Loan

12. _________ is a term used in accounting, economics and finance to spread the cost of an asset over the span of several years.

In simple words we can say that _________ is the reduction in the value of an asset due to usage, passage of time, wear and tear, technological outdating or obsolescence, depletion, inadequacy, rot, rust, decay or other such factors.

In accounting, _________ is a term used to describe any method of attributing the historical or purchase cost of an asset across its useful life, roughly corresponding to normal wear and tear.

a. General ledger
b. Net profit
c. Current asset
d. Depreciation

13. In financial accounting, a _________ is defined as an obligation of an entity arising from past transactions or events, the settlement of which may result in the transfer or use of assets, provision of services or other yielding of economic benefits in the future.

a. Corporate governance
b. Vested
c. False Claims Act
d. Liability

14. In economics, _________ or _________ goods or real _________ refers to factors of production used to create goods or services that are not themselves significantly consumed (though they may depreciate) in the production process. _________ goods may be acquired with money or financial _________. In finance and accounting, _________ generally refers to financial wealth, especially that used to start or maintain a business.

a. Vyborg Appeal
b. Screening
c. Disclosure
d. Capital

15. _________ is a company's financial statement that indicates how the revenue is transformed into the net income The purpose of the _________ is to show managers and investors whether the company made or lost money during the period being reported.

The important thing to remember about an _________ is that it represents a period of time.

a. AMEX
b. ABC Television Network
c. AIG
d. Income Statement

16. _________ means the giving out of information, either voluntarily or to be in compliance with legal regulations or workplace rules.

- In Computer security, full _________ means disclosing full information about vulnerabilities.
- In computing, _________ widget
- Journalism, full _________ refers to disclosing the interests of the writer which may bear on the subject being written about, for example, if the writer has worked with an interview subject in the past.

- In law:
  - The law of England and Wales, _________ refers to a process that may form part of legal proceedings, whereby parties inform to other parties the existence of any relevant documents that are, or have been, in their control. This compares with the process known as discovery in the course of legal proceedings in the United States.
  - In U.S. civil procedure (litigation rules for civil cases), _________ is a stage prior to trial. In civil cases, each party must disclose to the opposing party the following: names of witnesses which it may use to support its side, copies of documents (or mere description of these documents) in its control which it may use to support its side, computation of damages claimed, and certain insurance information. _________ is related to, but technically prior to, the discovery stage.
  - In Company law (known as 'corporate law' in the United States), _________ refers to giving out information about public or limited companies or their officers, which might be kept secret if the company was a private company or a partnership.

- In real property transactions, _________ refers to providing to a buyer information known to the seller or broker/agent concerning the condition or other aspects of real property that would affect the property's value or desirability. These rules regarding what information must be disclosed, and whether the information must be disclosed even if a buyer does not ask, vary from one jurisdiction to the next.

a. Tax harmonisation
b. Disclosure
c. Trailing
d. Controlled Foreign Corporations

17. _________ is a term used with respect to a retailed product, indicating that the product is in the end of its product lifetime and a vendor will no longer be marketing, selling, or promoting a particular product and may also be limiting or ending support for the product. In the specific case of product sales, the term end-of-sale (EOS) has also been used. The term lifetime, after the last production date, depends on the product and is related to a customer's expected product lifetime.

a. AIG
b. End-of-life
c. AMEX
d. ABC Television Network

18. _________ is the term used to refer to the standard framework of guidelines for financial accounting used in any given jurisdiction. _________ includes the standards, conventions, and rules accountants follow in recording and summarizing transactions, and in the preparation of financial statements.

Financial accounting information must be assembled and reported objectively.

a. Current asset
b. Generally accepted accounting principles
c. General ledger
d. Long-term liabilities

19. _________ of something is, in finance, the adding together of interest or different investments over a period of time such as atoms (1 - the act or process of accruing; 2 - the amount that accrues.) It holds specific meanings in accounting and payroll.

_________, in accounting, describes the accounting method known as _________ basis, whereby revenues and expenses are recognized when they are accrued, i.e. accumulated (earned or incurred), regardless when the actual cash is received or paid out.

a. Assets
b. Accounts receivable
c. Earnings before interest, taxes, depreciation and amortization
d. Accrual

20. _________ is a method of accounting whereby economic activities (rather than cash flow) of financial events are considered, because of two complementary principles, which (together) determine the point, at which expenses and revenues are recognized. According to revenue recognition principle, revenues are realized when earned, whether or not they are received in cash.
a. Accrual
b. Earnings before interest, taxes, depreciation and amortization
c. Accrued revenue
d. Accrual basis accounting

21. The term _________, derived from the distinctive T shape, is frequently used when discussing or analyzing accounting or business transactions. _________s are used to represent general ledger accounts.

Typically one or more Ts are drawn on a white board or blank piece of paper. A general ledger account name or number is then written above each T. Debit entries are recorded on the left side of the 'T' and credit entries are recorded on the right side of the 'T'.

a. T account
b. 3M Company
c. BMC Software, Inc.
d. BNSF Railway

22. In finance, _________ refers to the way a corporation finances its assets through some combination of equity, debt, or hybrid securities. A firm's _________ is then the composition or 'structure' of its liabilities. For example, a firm that sells $20 billion in equity and $80 billion in debt is said to be 20% equity-financed and 80% debt-financed.

a. Flow-through entity
b. Restricted stock
c. Gross income
d. Capital structure

23. _________ is a specific term used in companies' financial reporting from the company-whole point of view. Because that use excludes the effects of changing ownership interest, an economic measure of _________ is necessary for financial analysis from the shareholders' point of view

_________ is defined by the Financial Accounting Standards Board, or FASB, as 'the change in equity [net assets] of a business enterprise during a period from transactions and other events and circumstances from nonowner sources. It includes all changes in equity during a period except those resulting from investments by owners and distributions to owners.'

_________ is the sum of net income and other items that must bypass the income statement because they have not been realized, including items like an unrealized holding gain or loss from available for sale securities and foreign currency translation gains or losses.

a. 3M Company
b. BMC Software, Inc.
c. BNSF Railway
d. Comprehensive income

24. A _________ is a fungible, negotiable instrument representing financial value. they are broadly categorized into debt securities (such as banknotes, bonds and debentures), and equity securities; e.g., common stocks. The company or other entity issuing the _________ is called the issuer.

a. BMC Software, Inc.
b. Tracking stock
c. Security
d. 3M Company

25. The U.S. _________ is an independent agency of the United States government which holds primary responsibility for enforcing the federal securities laws and regulating the securities industry, the nation's stock and options exchanges, and other electronic securities markets. The SEC was created by section 4 of the Securities Exchange Act of 1934 (now codified as 15 U.S.C. ÂÂ§ 78d and commonly referred to as the 1934 Act.)

a. BNSF Railway
b. 3M Company
c. Securities and Exchange Commission
d. BMC Software, Inc.

26. _________ can be regarded as an outcome of mental processes (cognitive process) leading to the selection of a course of action among several alternatives. Every _________ process produces a final choice. The output can be an action or an opinion of choice.

a. BMC Software, Inc.
b. 3M Company
c. BNSF Railway
d. Decision making

27. _________ are the earnings returned on the initial investment amount.

In the US, the Financial Accounting Standards Board (FASB) requires companies' income statements to report _________ for each of the major categories of the income statement: continuing operations, discontinued operations, extraordinary items, and net income.

The _________ formula does not include preferred dividends for categories outside of continued operations and net income.

a. Average accounting return
b. Invested capital
c. Earnings per share
d. Earnings yield

28. The term '_________' refers to the concept of collecting information and attempting to spot a pattern in the information. In some fields of study, the term '_________' has more formally-defined meanings.

In project management _________ is a mathematical technique that uses historical results to predict future outcome.

a. 3M Company
b. Multicollinearity
c. Regression analysis
d. Trend analysis

29. _________ is a company's earnings per share (EPS) calculated using fully diluted shares outstanding. _________ indicates a 'worst case' scenario, one in which everyone who could have received stock without purchasing it directly for the full market value did so.

To find _________, basic EPS is calculated for each of the categories on the income statement first. Then each of the dilutive securities are ranked based on their effects, from most dilutive to least dilutive and antidilutive. Then the basic EPS number is diluted one by one by applying each one, skipping any instruments that have an antidilutive effect.

a. Diluted earnings per share
b. Financial ratio
c. Return on assets Du Pont
d. Cash conversion cycle

30. In mathematics, two elements x and y of a set partially ordered by a relation ≤ are said to be _________ if and only if x ≤ y or y ≤ x if and only if x < y or y < x or y = x. For example, two sets are _________ with respect to inclusion if and only if one is a subset of the other.

In a classification of mathematical objects such as topological spaces, two criteria are said to be _________ when the objects that obey one criterion constitute a subset of the objects that obey the other one .

a. Consumption
b. Scientific Research and Experimental Development Tax Incentive Program
c. Comparable
d. Database auditing

31. _________ is a financial ratio that measures the efficiency of a company's use of its assets in generating sales revenue or sales income to the company.

$$Asset\ Turnover = \frac{Sales}{AverageTotalAssets}$$

- 'Sales' is the value of 'Net Sales' or 'Sales' from the company's income statement
- 'Average Total Assets' is the value of 'Total assets' from the company's balance sheet in the beginning and the end of the fiscal period divided by 2.

a. Information ratio
b. Asset turnover
c. Average propensity to consume
d. Enterprise Value/Sales

32. _________ are formal records of a business' financial activities.

In British English, including United Kingdom company law, _________ are often referred to as accounts, although the term _________ is also used, particularly by accountants.

_________ provide an overview of a business' financial condition in both short and long term.

a. 3M Company
b. Financial statements
c. Notes to the financial statements
d. Statement of retained earnings

33. _________ is the balance of the amounts of cash being received and paid by a business during a defined period of time, sometimes tied to a specific project. Measurement of _________ can be used

- to evaluate the state or performance of a business or project.
- to determine problems with liquidity. Being profitable does not necessarily mean being liquid. A company can fail because of a shortage of cash, even while profitable.
- to project rate of returns. The time of _________s into and out of projects are used as inputs to financial models such as internal rate of return, and net present value.
- to examine income or growth of a business when it is believed that accrual accounting concepts do not represent economic realities. Alternately, _________ can be used to 'validate' the net income generated by accrual accounting.

_________ as a generic term may be used differently depending on context, and certain _________ definitions may be adapted by analysts and users for their own uses. Common terms include operating _________ and free _________.

a. Controlling interest
b. Commercial paper
c. Flow-through entity
d. Cash Flow

34. The _________ is a financial ratio that measures whether or not a firm has enough resources to pay its debts over the next 12 months. It compares a firm's current assets to its current liabilities. It is expressed as follows:

$$\text{Current ratio} = \frac{\text{Current Assets}}{\text{Current Liabilities}}$$

For example, if WXY Company's current assets are $50,000,000 and its current liabilities are $40,000,000, then its _________ would be $50,000,000 divided by $40,000,000, which equals 1.25.

a. Current ratio
b. Net Interest Income
c. Times interest earned
d. Return on capital

35. In financial accounting, a _________ or Statement of cash flows is a financial statement that shows a company's flow of cash. The money coming into the business is called cash inflow, and money going out from the business is called cash outflow. The statement shows how changes in balance sheet and income accounts affect cash and cash equivalents, and breaks the analysis down to operating, investing, and financing activities.
a. 3M Company
b. Cash flow statement
c. BMC Software, Inc.
d. BNSF Railway

36. _________ is one of the accounting liquidity ratios, a financial ratio. This ratio measures the number of times, on average, receivables (e.g. Accounts Receivable) are collected during the period. A popular variant of the _________ is to convert it into an Average Collection Period in terms of days.
a. Capital
b. Receivable turnover ratio
c. Shrinkage
d. Price-to-sales ratio

37. In finance, the _________ or quick ratio or liquid ratio measures the ability of a company to use its near cash or quick assets to immediately extinguish or retire its current liabilities. Quick assets include those current assets that presumably can be quickly converted to cash at close to their book values.

$$\text{Quick (Acid Test) Ratio} = \frac{\text{Cash} + \text{Marketable Securities} + \text{Accounts Receivables}}{\text{Current Liabilities}}$$

Generally, the acid test ratio should be 1:1 or better, however this varies widely by industry.

a. Earnings per share
b. Invested capital
c. Inventory turnover
d. Acid-test

38. In financial and business accounting, _________ is a measure of a firm's profitability that excludes interest and income tax expenses.

EBIT = Operating Revenue - Operating Expenses (OPEX) + Non-operating Income

Operating Income = Operating Revenue - Operating Expenses

Operating income is the difference between operating revenues and operating expenses, but it is also sometimes used as a synonym for EBIT and operating profit. This is true if the firm has no non-operating income.

a. AMEX
b. AIG
c. ABC Television Network
d. Earnings before interest and taxes

39. _________ is a fee paid on borrowed assets. It is the price paid for the use of borrowed money , or, money earned by deposited funds .Assets that are sometimes lent with _________ include money, shares, consumer goods through hire purchase, major assets such as aircraft, and even entire factories in finance lease arrangements. The _________ is calculated upon the value of the assets in the same manner as upon money.
a. Interest
b. AIG
c. Insolvency
d. ABC Television Network

40. _________ or interest coverage ratio is a measure of a company's ability to honor its debt payments. It may be calculated as either EBIT or EBITDA divided by the total interest payable.

>

a. Capital recovery factor
b. Times interest earned
c. Yield Gap
d. Return of capital

41. A _________ is an annual report required by the U.S. Securities and Exchange Commission (SEC), that gives a comprehensive summary of a public company's performance. Although similarly named, the annual report on _________ is distinct from the often glossy 'annual report to shareholders', which a company must send to its shareholders when it holds an annual meeting to elect directors (though some companies combine the annual report and the 10-K into one document.) The 10-K includes information such as company history, organizational structure, executive compensation, equity, subsidiaries, and audited financial statements, among other information.
a. Form 10-K
b. 3M Company
c. Form 8-K
d. Form 10-Q

1. _________ is the balance of the amounts of cash being received and paid by a business during a defined period of time, sometimes tied to a specific project. Measurement of _________ can be used

- to evaluate the state or performance of a business or project.
- to determine problems with liquidity. Being profitable does not necessarily mean being liquid. A company can fail because of a shortage of cash, even while profitable.
- to project rate of returns. The time of _________s into and out of projects are used as inputs to financial models such as internal rate of return, and net present value.
- to examine income or growth of a business when it is believed that accrual accounting concepts do not represent economic realities. Alternately, _________ can be used to 'validate' the net income generated by accrual accounting.

_________ as a generic term may be used differently depending on context, and certain _________ definitions may be adapted by analysts and users for their own uses. Common terms include operating _________ and free _________.

a. Commercial paper
b. Cash Flow
c. Controlling interest
d. Flow-through entity

2. _________ is a company's financial statement that indicates how the revenue is transformed into the net income The purpose of the _________ is to show managers and investors whether the company made or lost money during the period being reported.

The important thing to remember about an _________ is that it represents a period of time.

a. AMEX
b. Income Statement
c. ABC Television Network
d. AIG

3. In financial accounting, a _________ or Statement of cash flows is a financial statement that shows a company's flow of cash. The money coming into the business is called cash inflow, and money going out from the business is called cash outflow. The statement shows how changes in balance sheet and income accounts affect cash and cash equivalents, and breaks the analysis down to operating, investing, and financing activities.
a. 3M Company
b. BNSF Railway
c. Cash flow statement
d. BMC Software, Inc.

4. _________ of something is, in finance, the adding together of interest or different investments over a period of time such as atoms (1 - the act or process of accruing; 2 - the amount that accrues.) It holds specific meanings in accounting and payroll.

_________, in accounting, describes the accounting method known as _________ basis, whereby revenues and expenses are recognized when they are accrued, i.e. accumulated (earned or incurred), regardless when the actual cash is received or paid out.

a. Earnings before interest, taxes, depreciation and amortization
b. Assets
c. Accounts receivable
d. Accrual

5. _________ is a method of accounting whereby economic activities (rather than cash flow) of financial events are considered, because of two complementary principles, which (together) determine the point, at which expenses and revenues are recognized. According to revenue recognition principle, revenues are realized when earned, whether or not they are received in cash.
a. Accrual basis accounting
b. Accrual
c. Accrued revenue
d. Earnings before interest, taxes, depreciation and amortization

6. _________ is a method of accounting whereby cash flow of financial events is considered. The method recognizes revenues when cash is received and recognizes expenses when cash is paid out. In cash accounting, revenues and expenses are also called cash receipts and cash payments respectively.
a. Cash basis accounting
b. Closing entries
c. Net sales
d. Treasury stock

7. In financial accounting, _________ , cash flow provided by operations or cash flow from operating activities, refers to the amount of cash a company generates from the revenues it brings in, excluding costs associated with long-term investment on capital items or investment in securities.

_________ = Cash generated from operations less taxation and interest paid, investment income received and less dividends paid gives rise to _________s per International Financial Reporting Standards.

To calculate cash generated from operations, one must calculate cash generated from customers and cash paid to suppliers.

a. ABC Television Network
b. AIG
c. AMEX
d. Operating cash flow

8. In economics, the _________, (or _________) measures the payments that flow between any individual country and all other countries. It is used to summarize all international economic transactions for that country during a specific time period, usually a year. The _________ is determined by the country's exports and imports of goods, services, and financial capital, as well as financial transfers.
a. Balance of payments
b. Moving average
c. Stock split
d. Yield to maturity

9. _________ is that which is owed; usually referencing assets owed, but the term can also cover moral obligations and other interactions not requiring money. In the case of assets, _________ is a means of using future purchasing power in the present before a summation has been earned. Some companies and corporations use _________ as a part of their overall corporate finance strategy.
a. Lender
b. Debenture
c. Debt
d. Loan

10. _________ is a financial ratio that indicates the percentage of a company's assets are provided via debt. It is the ratio of total debt (the sum of current liabilities and long-term liabilities) and total assets (the sum of current assets, fixed assets, and other assets such as 'goodwill'.)

$$\text{Debt ratio} = \frac{\text{Total Debt}}{\text{Total Assets}}$$

or alternatively:

$$\text{Debt ratio} = \frac{\text{Total Liability}}{\text{Total Assets}}$$

For example, a company with $2 million in total assets and $500,000 in total liabilities would have a _________ of 25%

Like all financial ratios, a company's _________ should be compared with their industry average or other competing firms.

a. Debt ratio
b. 3M Company
c. Profitability index
d. Finance lease

11. The _________, sometimes known as the nominal ledger, is the main accounting record of a business which uses double-entry bookkeeping. It will usually include accounts for such items as current assets, fixed assets, liabilities, revenue and expense items, gains and losses.

The _________ is a collection of the group of accounts that supports the items shown in the major financial statements.

a. Sales journal
b. General ledger
c. Journal entry
d. General journal

1. An _________ is a comprehensive report on a company's activities throughout the preceding year. _________s are intended to give shareholders and other interested persons information about the company's activities and financial performance. Most jurisdictions require companies to prepare and disclose _________s, and many require the _________ to be filed at the company's registry.

a. AIG
b. Annual Report
c. ABC Television Network
d. AMEX

2. A _________ is an annual report required by the U.S. Securities and Exchange Commission (SEC), that gives a comprehensive summary of a public company's performance. Although similarly named, the annual report on _________ is distinct from the often glossy 'annual report to shareholders', which a company must send to its shareholders when it holds an annual meeting to elect directors (though some companies combine the annual report and the 10-K into one document.) The 10-K includes information such as company history, organizational structure, executive compensation, equity, subsidiaries, and audited financial statements, among other information.

a. Form 10-Q
b. 3M Company
c. Form 10-K
d. Form 8-K

3. A _________ is a fungible, negotiable instrument representing financial value. they are broadly categorized into debt securities (such as banknotes, bonds and debentures), and equity securities; e.g., common stocks. The company or other entity issuing the _________ is called the issuer.

a. Tracking stock
b. 3M Company
c. Security
d. BMC Software, Inc.

4. The U.S. _________ is an independent agency of the United States government which holds primary responsibility for enforcing the federal securities laws and regulating the securities industry, the nation's stock and options exchanges, and other electronic securities markets. The SEC was created by section 4 of the Securities Exchange Act of 1934 (now codified as 15 U.S.C. ÂÂ§ 78d and commonly referred to as the 1934 Act.)

a. BMC Software, Inc.
b. Securities and Exchange Commission
c. BNSF Railway
d. 3M Company

5. _________ is the balance of the amounts of cash being received and paid by a business during a defined period of time, sometimes tied to a specific project. Measurement of _________ can be used

- to evaluate the state or performance of a business or project.
- to determine problems with liquidity. Being profitable does not necessarily mean being liquid. A company can fail because of a shortage of cash, even while profitable.
- to project rate of returns. The time of _________s into and out of projects are used as inputs to financial models such as internal rate of return, and net present value.
- to examine income or growth of a business when it is believed that accrual accounting concepts do not represent economic realities. Alternately, _________ can be used to 'validate' the net income generated by accrual accounting.

_________ as a generic term may be used differently depending on context, and certain _________ definitions may be adapted by analysts and users for their own uses. Common terms include operating _________ and free _________.

a. Controlling interest
b. Commercial paper
c. Flow-through entity
d. Cash Flow

6. A _________ is a party (e.g. person, organization, company, or government) that has a claim to the services of a second party. It is a person or institution to whom money is owed. The first party, in general, has provided some property or service to the second party under the assumption (usually enforced by contract) that the second party will return an equivalent property or service.
a. Treasury company
b. Payback period
c. Par value
d. Creditor

7. In financial accounting, a _________ or Statement of cash flows is a financial statement that shows a company's flow of cash. The money coming into the business is called cash inflow, and money going out from the business is called cash outflow. The statement shows how changes in balance sheet and income accounts affect cash and cash equivalents, and breaks the analysis down to operating, investing, and financing activities.
a. BNSF Railway
b. BMC Software, Inc.
c. Cash flow statement
d. 3M Company

8. _________ of a business involves analyzing its financial statements and health, its management and competitive advantages, and its competitors and markets. The term is used to distinguish such analysis from other types of investment analysis, such as quantitative analysis and technical analysis.

_________ is performed on historical and present data, but with the goal of making financial forecasts.

a. 3M Company
b. BMC Software, Inc.
c. BNSF Railway
d. Fundamental analysis

9. _________ is concerned with the provisions and use of accounting information to managers within organizations, to provide them with the basis to make informed business decisions that will allow them to be better equipped in their management and control functions.

In contrast to financial accountancy information, _________ information is:

- usually confidential and used by management, instead of publicly reported;
- forward-looking, instead of historical;
- pragmatically computed using extensive management information systems and internal controls, instead of complying with accounting standards.

This is because of the different emphasis: _________ information is used within an organization, typically for decision-making.

a. Governmental accounting
b. Nonassurance services
c. Management accounting
d. Grenzplankostenrechnung

10. In economics, _________ or _________ goods or real _________ refers to factors of production used to create goods or services that are not themselves significantly consumed (though they may depreciate) in the production process. _________ goods may be acquired with money or financial _________. In finance and accounting, _________ generally refers to financial wealth, especially that used to start or maintain a business.
a. Screening
b. Capital
c. Vyborg Appeal
d. Disclosure

11. In finance, _________ refers to the way a corporation finances its assets through some combination of equity, debt, or hybrid securities. A firm's _________ is then the composition or 'structure' of its liabilities. For example, a firm that sells $20 billion in equity and $80 billion in debt is said to be 20% equity-financed and 80% debt-financed.

a. Capital structure
b. Flow-through entity
c. Gross income
d. Restricted stock

12. _________ is that which is owed; usually referencing assets owed, but the term can also cover moral obligations and other interactions not requiring money. In the case of assets, _________ is a means of using future purchasing power in the present before a summation has been earned. Some companies and corporations use _________ as a part of their overall corporate finance strategy.

a. Loan
b. Lender
c. Debt
d. Debenture

13. _________ is the state or fact of exclusive rights and control over property, which may be an object, land/real estate or intellectual property. An _________ right is also referred to as title.

_________ is the key building block in the development of the capitalist socio-economic system.

a. Encumbrance
b. Administrative proceeding
c. Ownership
d. ABC Television Network

14. A _________ is used in research to outline possible courses of action or to present a preferred approach to an idea or thought. For example, the philosopher Isaiah Berlin used the 'hedgehogs' versus 'foxes' approach; a 'hedgehog' might approach the world in terms of a single organizing principle; a 'fox' might pursue multiple conflicting goals simultaneously. Alternatively, an empiricist might approach a subject by direct examination, whereas an intuitionist might simply intuit what's next.

a. 3M Company
b. Conceptual Framework
c. BNSF Railway
d. BMC Software, Inc.

15. A _________ has several related meanings:

- a daily record of events or business; a private _________ is usually referred to as a diary.
- a newspaper or other periodical, in the literal sense of one published each day;
- many publications issued at stated intervals, such as magazines, or scholarly academic _________s, or the record of the transactions of a society, are often called _________s. Although _________ is sometimes used, erroneously, as a synonym for 'magazine,' in academic use, a _________ refers to a serious, scholarly publication, most often peer-reviewed. A non-scholarly magazine written for an educated audience about an industry or an area of professional activity is usually called a professional magazine.

The word 'journalist' for one whose business is writing for the public press has been in use since the end of the 17th century.

Open access _________s are scholarly _________s that are available to the reader without financial or other barrier other than access to the internet itself. Some are subsidized, and some require payment on behalf of the author. Subsidized _________s are financed by an academic institution or a government information center.

a. BMC Software, Inc.
b. BNSF Railway
c. 3M Company
d. Journal

16. In accounting, _________ or sales profit is the difference between revenue and the cost of making a product or providing a service, before deducting overhead, payroll, taxation, and interest payments. Note that this is different from operating profit (earnings before interest and taxes.)

Net sales are calculated:

Net sales = Sales - Sales returns and allowances.

a. Commercial paper
b. Participating preferred stock
c. Capital structure
d. Gross profit

17. _________ is a financial ratio used to assess the profitability of a firm's core activities, excluding fixed costs.

The general calculation is:

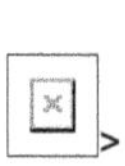

The _________ is related to the net profit margin, which assesses the profitability of an organization after including fixed costs.

_________ indicates the relationship between net sales revenue and the cost of goods sold.

a. Gross income
b. Commercial paper
c. Participating preferred stock
d. Gross profit margin

18. In bookkeeping, accounting, and finance, _________ are operating revenues earned by a company when it sells its products. Revenue (_________) are reported directly on the income statement as Sales or _________.

In financial ratios that use income statement sales values, 'sales' refers to _________, not gross sales.

a. Deferred
b. Matching principle
c. Historical cost
d. Net sales

19. _________, net margin, net _________ or net profit ratio all refer to a measure of profitability. It is calculated by finding the net profit as a percentage of the revenue.

$$\text{Net profit margin} = \frac{\text{Net profit (after taxes)}}{\text{Revenue}} \times 100$$

The _________ is mostly used for internal comparison.

a. BMC Software, Inc.
b. 3M Company
c. BNSF Railway
d. Profit margin

20. A _________ is the pinnacle activity involved in selling products or services in return for money or other compensation. It is an act of completion of a commercial activity.

A _________ is completed by the seller, the owner of the goods.

a. Sale
b. Tertiary sector of economy
c. High yield stock
d. Maturity

21. In business and finance accounting, _________ is equal to the gross profit minus overheads minus interest payable plus/minus one off items for a given time period (usually: accounting period.)

A common synonym for '_________' when discussing financial statements (which include a balance sheet and an income statement) is the bottom line. This term results from the traditional appearance of an income statement which shows all allocated revenues and expenses over a specified time period with the resulting summation on the bottom line of the report.

a. Salvage value
b. Treasury stock
c. Net profit
d. Cost of goods sold

22. In business and accounting, _________ are everything of value that is owned by a person or company. It is a claim on the property your income of a borrower. The balance sheet of a firm records the monetary value of the _________ owned by the firm.

a. Accounts receivable
b. Earnings before interest, taxes, depreciation and amortization
c. Accrual basis accounting
d. Assets

23. In financial accounting, a _________ or statement of financial position is a summary of a person's or organization's balances. Assets, liabilities and ownership equity are listed as of a specific date, such as the end of its financial year. A _________ is often described as a snapshot of a company's financial condition.

a. Financial statements
b. Statement of retained earnings
c. 3M Company
d. Balance Sheet

24. In finance, _________ also known as return on investment, rate of profit or sometimes just return, is the ratio of money gained or lost on an investment relative to the amount of money invested. The amount of money gained or lost may be referred to as interest, profit/loss, gain/loss, or net income/loss. The money invested may be referred to as the asset, capital, principal, or the cost basis of the investment.

a. Debt to capital ratio
b. Rate of return
c. Theoretical ex-rights price
d. Capital employed

25. The _________ percentage shows how profitable a company's assets are in generating revenue.

_________ can be computed as:

$$\text{ROA} = \frac{\text{Net Income - Interest Expense - Interest Tax savings}}{\text{Average Total Assets}}$$

This number tells you what the company can do with what it has, i.e. how many dollars of earnings they derive from each dollar of assets they control. Its a useful number for comparing competing companies in the same industry.

a. Return on sales
b. Return on assets
c. Capital employed
d. Statutory Liquidity Ratio

26. _________ are payments made by a corporation to its shareholder members. It is the portion of corporate profits paid out to stockholders. When a corporation earns a profit or surplus, that money can be put to two uses: it can either be re-invested in the business (called retained earnings), or it can be paid to the shareholders as a dividend.

a. Dividend stripping
b. Dividend yield
c. Dividend payout ratio
d. Dividends

27. _________ is the fraction of net income a firm pays to its stockholders in dividends:

The part of the earnings not paid to investors is left for investment to provide for future earnings growth. Investors seeking high current income and limited capital growth prefer companies with high _________. However investors seeking capital growth may prefer lower payout ratio because capital gains are taxed at a lower rate.

a. Dividend yield
b. Dividends
c. Dividend stripping
d. Dividend payout ratio

28. The _________ is a financial ratio indicating the relative proportion of equity to all used to finance a company's assets. The two components are often taken from the firm's balance sheet or statement of financial position (so-called book value), but the ratio may also be calculated using market values for both, if the company's equities are publicly traded.

The _________ is especially in Central Europe a very common financial ratio while in the US the debt to _________ is more often used in financial (research) reports.

a. Efficiency ratio
b. Earnings yield
c. Average accounting return
d. Equity ratio

29. _________ is a specific term used in companies' financial reporting from the company-whole point of view. Because that use excludes the effects of changing ownership interest, an economic measure of _________ is necessary for financial analysis from the shareholders' point of view

_________ is defined by the Financial Accounting Standards Board, or FASB, as 'the change in equity [net assets] of a business enterprise during a period from transactions and other events and circumstances from nonowner sources. It includes all changes in equity during a period except those resulting from investments by owners and distributions to owners.'

_________ is the sum of net income and other items that must bypass the income statement because they have not been realized, including items like an unrealized holding gain or loss from available for sale securities and foreign currency translation gains or losses.

a. Comprehensive income
b. BNSF Railway
c. BMC Software, Inc.
d. 3M Company

30. _________ are the earnings returned on the initial investment amount.

In the US, the Financial Accounting Standards Board (FASB) requires companies' income statements to report _________ for each of the major categories of the income statement: continuing operations, discontinued operations, extraordinary items, and net income.

The _________ formula does not include preferred dividends for categories outside of continued operations and net income.

a. Invested capital
b. Average accounting return
c. Earnings yield
d. Earnings per share

31. The _________, a ratio that is typically applied to banks, in simple terms is defined as expenses as a percentage of revenue (expenses / revenue), with a few variations. A lower percentage is better since that means expenses are low and earnings are high. It is related to operating leverage, which measures the ratio between fixed costs and variable costs.
a. Efficiency ratio
b. Equity ratio
c. Operating leverage
d. Average rate of return

32. _________ is a financial ratio that measures the efficiency of a company's use of its assets in generating sales revenue or sales income to the company.

$$Asset\ Turnover = \frac{Sales}{AverageTotalAssets}$$

- 'Sales' is the value of 'Net Sales' or 'Sales' from the company's income statement
- 'Average Total Assets' is the value of 'Total assets' from the company's balance sheet in the beginning and the end of the fiscal period divided by 2.

a. Information ratio
b. Average propensity to consume
c. Enterprise Value/Sales
d. Asset turnover

33. _________ is one of the accounting liquidity ratios, a financial ratio. This ratio measures the number of times, on average, receivables (e.g. Accounts Receivable) are collected during the period. A popular variant of the _________ is to convert it into an Average Collection Period in terms of days.

a. Price-to-sales ratio
b. Shrinkage
c. Capital
d. Receivable turnover ratio

34. The _________ is an equation that equals the cost of goods sold divided by the average inventory. Average inventory equals beginning inventory plus ending inventory divided by 2.

The formula for _________:

$$\text{Inventory Turnover} = \frac{\text{Cost of Goods Sold}}{\text{Average Inventory}}$$

The formula for average inventory:

$$\text{Average Inventory} = \frac{\text{Beginning inventory+Ending inventory}}{2}$$

A low turnover rate may point to overstocking, obsolescence, or deficiencies in the product line or marketing effort.

a. Inventory turnover
b. Enterprise Value/Sales
c. Earnings per share
d. Upside potential ratio

35. _________ is one of the Accounting Liquidity ratios, a financial ratio. This ratio measures the number of times, on average, the inventory is sold during the period. Its purpose is to measure the liquidity of the inventory.

a. AIG
b. Inventory turnover ratio
c. Ending inventory
d. ABC Television Network

36. The _________ is a financial ratio that measures whether or not a firm has enough resources to pay its debts over the next 12 months. It compares a firm's current assets to its current liabilities. It is expressed as follows:

$$\text{Current ratio} = \frac{\text{Current Assets}}{\text{Current Liabilities}}$$

For example, if WXY Company's current assets are $50,000,000 and its current liabilities are $40,000,000, then its _________ would be $50,000,000 divided by $40,000,000, which equals 1.25.

a. Times interest earned
b. Current ratio
c. Return on capital
d. Net Interest Income

37. _________ is a business, economics or investment term that refers to an asset's ability to be easily converted through an act of buying or selling without causing a significant movement in the price and with minimum loss of value. Money, or cash on hand, is the most liquid asset. An act of exchange of a less liquid asset with a more liquid asset is called liquidation.

a. Transfer agent
b. Spot rate
c. Financial instruments
d. Market liquidity

38. In finance, the _________ or quick ratio or liquid ratio measures the ability of a company to use its near cash or quick assets to immediately extinguish or retire its current liabilities. Quick assets include those current assets that presumably can be quickly converted to cash at close to their book values.

$$\text{Quick (Acid Test) Ratio} = \frac{\text{Cash} + \text{Marketable Securities} + \text{Accounts Receivables}}{\text{Current Liabilities}}$$

Generally, the acid test ratio should be 1:1 or better, however this varies widely by industry.

a. Earnings per share
b. Invested capital
c. Inventory turnover
d. Acid-test

39. In financial accounting, _________, cash flow provided by operations or cash flow from operating activities, refers to the amount of cash a company generates from the revenues it brings in, excluding costs associated with long-term investment on capital items or investment in securities.

_________ = Cash generated from operations less taxation and interest paid, investment income received and less dividends paid gives rise to _________s per International Financial Reporting Standards.

To calculate cash generated from operations, one must calculate cash generated from customers and cash paid to suppliers.

a. ABC Television Network
b. Operating cash flow
c. AMEX
d. AIG

40. A _________, or simply proprietorship is a type of business entity which legally has no separate existence from its owner. Hence, the limitations of liability enjoyed by a corporation and limited liability partnerships do not apply to sole proprietors. All debts of the business are debts of the owner.

a. Sole proprietorship
b. Time to market
c. Customer satisfaction
d. Free cash flow

41. In economics, the _________, (or _________) measures the payments that flow between any individual country and all other countries. It is used to summarize all international economic transactions for that country during a specific time period, usually a year. The _________ is determined by the country's exports and imports of goods, services, and financial capital, as well as financial transfers.

a. Yield to maturity
b. Stock split
c. Balance of payments
d. Moving average

42. _________ is a financial ratio that indicates the percentage of a company's assets are provided via debt. It is the ratio of total debt (the sum of current liabilities and long-term liabilities) and total assets (the sum of current assets, fixed assets, and other assets such as 'goodwill'.)

$$\text{Debt ratio} = \frac{\text{Total Debt}}{\text{Total Assets}}$$

or alternatively:

$$\text{Debt ratio} = \frac{\text{Total Liability}}{\text{Total Assets}}$$

For example, a company with $2 million in total assets and $500,000 in total liabilities would have a _________ of 25%

Like all financial ratios, a company's _________ should be compared with their industry average or other competing firms.

a. 3M Company
b. Finance lease
c. Debt ratio
d. Profitability index

43. The _________, sometimes known as the nominal ledger, is the main accounting record of a business which uses double-entry bookkeeping. It will usually include accounts for such items as current assets, fixed assets, liabilities, revenue and expense items, gains and losses.

The _________ is a collection of the group of accounts that supports the items shown in the major financial statements.

a. Sales journal
b. General journal
c. Journal entry
d. General ledger

44. A sole _________, or simply _________ is a type of business entity which legally has no separate existence from its owner. Hence, the limitations of liability enjoyed by a corporation and limited liability partnerships do not apply to sole proprietors. All debts of the business are debts of the owner.
a. Free cash flow
b. Pre-determined overhead rate
c. Proprietorship
d. Safety stock

45. In finance, or business _________ is the ability of an entity to pay its debts with available cash. _________ can also be described as the ability of a corporation to meet its long-term fixed expenses and to accomplish long-term expansion and growth. The better a company's _________, the better it is financially.

a. Capital asset
b. BMC Software, Inc.
c. 3M Company
d. Solvency

46. _________ and credit are formal bookkeeping and accounting terms. They are the most fundamental concepts in accounting, representing the two records that one party in a transaction makes on its records, transferring a money balance from one account to another, one representing a reduction of liability or increase in asset, and the other representing a balancing increase in liability or reduction of asset.

Introduction

_________s and credits are a system of notation used in accounting to keep track of money movements (transactions) into and out of an account.

a. Debit and credit
b. Bookkeeping
c. Cookie jar accounting
d. Debit

47. _________ is a fee paid on borrowed assets. It is the price paid for the use of borrowed money , or, money earned by deposited funds .Assets that are sometimes lent with _________ include money, shares, consumer goods through hire purchase, major assets such as aircraft, and even entire factories in finance lease arrangements. The _________ is calculated upon the value of the assets in the same manner as upon money.
a. ABC Television Network
b. AIG
c. Insolvency
d. Interest

48. _________ or interest coverage ratio is a measure of a company's ability to honor its debt payments. It may be calculated as either EBIT or EBITDA divided by the total interest payable.

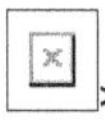

a. Capital recovery factor
b. Times interest earned
c. Return of capital
d. Yield Gap

49. _________ is a mathematical science pertaining to the collection, analysis, interpretation or explanation, and presentation of data. It also provides tools for prediction and forecasting based on data. It is applicable to a wide variety of academic disciplines, from the natural and social sciences to the humanities, government and business.
a. Time series
b. Variance
c. Probability distribution
d. Statistics

50. The general definition of an _________ is an evaluation of a person, organization, system, process, project or product. _________s are performed to ascertain the validity and reliability of information; also to provide an assessment of a system's internal control. The goal of an _________ is to express an opinion on the person/organization/system (etc) in question, under evaluation based on work done on a test basis.
a. Institute of Chartered Accountants of India
b. Audit regime
c. Assurance service
d. Audit

Chapter 1

1. a	2. d	3. d	4. b	5. d	6. d	7. d	8. b	9. d	10. d
11. b	12. b	13. d	14. d	15. a	16. d	17. c	18. d	19. d	20. a
21. d	22. a	23. c	24. c	25. b	26. a	27. c	28. b	29. a	30. a
31. b	32. d	33. d	34. d	35. c	36. d	37. d	38. d	39. d	40. d
41. b	42. b	43. d	44. b	45. d	46. c	47. c	48. a	49. d	50. d
51. a	52. d	53. d	54. b	55. d					

Chapter 2

1. d	2. a	3. b	4. a	5. b	6. b	7. d	8. b	9. d	10. c
11. c	12. d	13. d	14. d	15. b	16. d	17. c	18. c	19. d	20. d
21. c	22. d	23. d	24. a	25. d					

Chapter 3

1. d	2. c	3. a	4. d	5. d	6. a	7. d	8. c	9. d	10. b
11. a	12. a	13. c	14. d	15. a	16. d	17. d	18. d	19. b	20. d
21. d	22. c	23. b	24. b	25. a	26. c	27. b	28. d	29. d	30. a
31. d	32. c	33. d	34. d	35. b	36. b	37. d	38. b	39. c	40. d
41. c	42. d	43. d	44. d	45. d	46. b	47. d			

Chapter 4

1. d	2. d	3. b	4. c	5. d	6. d	7. d	8. d	9. d	10. c
11. b	12. d	13. d	14. d	15. b	16. a	17. b	18. d	19. d	20. a
21. a	22. d	23. d	24. d	25. d	26. d	27. b	28. c	29. d	30. a
31. b	32. d	33. b	34. c	35. b	36. c	37. d	38. c	39. d	40. d
41. a	42. b	43. d	44. d	45. a	46. c	47. d			

Chapter 5

1. d	2. d	3. d	4. c	5. d	6. d	7. d	8. c	9. c	10. b
11. d	12. d	13. c	14. d	15. c	16. d	17. d	18. d	19. a	20. d
21. d	22. c	23. d	24. a						

Chapter 6

1. d	2. a	3. b	4. c	5. d	6. a	7. b	8. d	9. a	10. d
11. b	12. a	13. b	14. d	15. d	16. d	17. d	18. d	19. b	20. d
21. d	22. d	23. a	24. a	25. d	26. d	27. a	28. a	29. d	30. b
31. c	32. c	33. c	34. b	35. b	36. d	37. d	38. d	39. d	

Chapter 7

1. a	2. c	3. a	4. d	5. a	6. b	7. a	8. d	9. b	10. a
11. d	12. d	13. d	14. b	15. b	16. a	17. d	18. d	19. d	20. a
21. d	22. d	23. b	24. b	25. a	26. c	27. b	28. c	29. c	

Chapter 8

1. d	2. d	3. b	4. b	5. a	6. c	7. c	8. b	9. b	10. d
11. a	12. d	13. c	14. a	15. b	16. d	17. c	18. d	19. a	20. d

Chapter 9

1. d	2. b	3. d	4. a	5. d	6. d	7. a	8. d	9. d	10. b
11. c	12. d	13. d	14. d	15. d	16. b	17. b	18. b	19. d	20. d
21. a	22. d	23. d	24. c	25. c	26. d	27. c	28. d	29. a	30. c
31. b	32. b	33. d	34. a	35. b	36. b	37. d	38. d	39. a	40. b
41. a									

Chapter 10

1. b	2. b	3. c	4. d	5. a	6. a	7. d	8. a	9. c	10. a
11. b									

Chapter 11

1. b	2. c	3. c	4. b	5. d	6. d	7. c	8. d	9. c	10. b
11. a	12. c	13. c	14. b	15. d	16. d	17. d	18. d	19. d	20. a
21. c	22. d	23. d	24. b	25. b	26. d	27. d	28. d	29. a	30. d
31. a	32. d	33. d	34. a	35. b	36. b	37. d	38. d	39. b	40. a
41. c	42. c	43. d	44. c	45. d	46. d	47. d	48. b	49. d	50. d

www.ingramcontent.com/pod-product-compliance
Lightning Source LLC
Chambersburg PA
CBHW082047230426
43670CB00016B/2802